TO PADDLE MY FEET

One woman's uplifting true account
of finding freedom against all odds

RITA SANDFORD

THIS BOOK IS DEDICATED TO:

My birth mother, who I don't remember, but is in my heart.

My father, who had to cope with so much.

My stepmother, who brought us together as a family.

Stuart, my brother, who I no longer remember, but loved as a brother.

Pauline, who was my constant friend during my time in hospital.

An unknown young girl from my early days in hospital – we shared hard times together.

Tim, my boyfriend, who has given me so much love and support over the years.

And all my friends for the good times we share.

I would also like to thank:
Lynne Nash
Joan El Faghloumi
for all their help with this book.

I want to climb catlike up cliffs
Fly on a zip wire like an eagle
Go down mines and feel
The bones of the earth.

I want to dive with a dolphin
Float like a red emperor
Tread along the seashore
With a foot in the waves.

I want to lie on my back
And stargaze for a night.
Touch a moonbeam
And taste the wind.

I need to run through long grass
Roll down sand dunes
Race a pack of wolves
And sleep a night away.

I want to climb a mast
Walk out on the yardarms.
Wander through a forest
And kick up piles of leaves.

But I can dream all my dreams
Relive all my adventures
Then if my body cannot do them
My mind can make them true.

~~~~

© Annie Goodhall

FOREWORD

No-one expects to become disabled at any age. When it happens, lives are changed forever. My life certainly changed forever. I think it's harder for a young child; I had to sit and watch while other children ran around and played. I felt isolated.

Many places weren't accessible so I rarely travelled anywhere. I watched while teenagers found boyfriends, went to parties and discos.

In the fifties and sixties, all disabled children were put into institutions or special schools, distanced from everything. We were hidden away so that the rest of society could get on with their lives. Education was basic; there was no need to teach disabled children when they remained hidden for most of their lives, taken care of by the Government.

Out of sight.

No-one ever expected to see a disabled person in the community. It was unthinkable.

Other adults asked my stepmother how I was. They heard her views from her perspective, never mine. I sat and listened to their conversations, saying 'I'm fine' if anyone did think to ask me. I was never consulted or expected to respond. We all know the saying: Children should be seen and not heard.

I was earmarked to go to a special school after my stay in hospital, but my parents were determined that I should try to lead an ordinary life. The Education Authority didn't want to co-operate. There wasn't the support from Social Services as there is now.

As a disabled child, I finally had to fit into a new family – my father had remarried. I had to cope with my newly acquired disability: I'd been completely paralysed and only had some strength in my arms, but I was still expected to walk using any means. The aim was to get disabled people up and walking so that they could somehow fit into society. I was often in pain from trying to achieve this. The struggle was relentless.

To the outside world, we were a happy family who everyone admired. They couldn't see the cracks. It was like wallpapering over a broken wall; the surface looked good but we were all struggling in our own way. We were four people living under one roof, but I always felt as though I was on my own.

Now I'm an adult, I've learnt to speak up for myself. I know what I want. Most of my story has stayed hidden for years. It's my time to tell you what my life was really like.

Rita Sandford

I'd like to explain why I have named my book *To Paddle My Feet*.

Throughout my life, I've been fascinated by the sea, and especially the seashore. In my mind, I feel that it must be the most fabulous thing to wander along the shoreline with bare feet, the gentle rippling water running between my toes. I do envy other people doing this so casually; it is the one thing I find difficult to do, as sandy or pebbly beaches are not suitable for wheelchairs.

If there is any opportunity when I can get to the water's edge, then I have to paddle my feet. My friends know this and have often helped me achieve this over the years. It's a wonderful feeling!

CHAPTER 1

Early Years

I have no recollection of my life up until the age of five. It's as though I am looking at a blank wall. I often wonder what memories other people have. With me, there is nothing. Can I just not remember? Or, did my mind wipe it clean, as I had to cope with my new life after I became five?

I look at photo albums. I have photos of my birth mother, and she's looking happy. I can't remember her. I long to glimpse just one moment of us together. I rub my finger over her face in the hope that my memory stirs, but there's nothing. It is just a face looking back at me. I know she is my mother by the writing underneath.

I think one of the hardest things to happen to a young child is losing their mother. A mother is there for love, support and guidance. I missed all of that and had to cope the best way I could.

There are other people in the photos: my father, my brother Stuart, my grandparents and my cousins. Although my father said that his father spoilt me, I have to believe him as there is no memory of either set of grandparents. My cousins tell me that we lived a happy life; they used to come and visit. Margaret, my oldest cousin, can remember pushing me along the street in the pram. My birth mother had three sisters: Hilda, Olive, Gladys, and my mother Frances was the youngest. There are photos of us on outings together looking happy.

My father followed in his own father's footsteps and worked for the Great Western Railway, which was mainly steam trains when I was young. We could travel free and there are photos of us building sandcastles and playing in the sea.

You'd think I could've asked my father about my mother. He should remember everything we did together. On the odd occasion when I asked him, I could see the pain in his eyes as he tried to think of something to say. I could feel his hurt as he turned away from me. Yes, he could remember but it was too painful for him. He could stay composed if he said nothing. I wasn't going to learn anything from him.

Stuart was four years older than me. We played together as brother and sister when we were younger but it changed when I became five.

Our family was torn apart.

Then, after nearly two years of separation, Stuart and I didn't know what to say to each other. We were strangers who happened to be brother and sister. It was some years before we felt at ease with each other's company. I always thought we had a lifetime together to talk about these things, but that wasn't to be.

I was born in Cyril Street, a terrace house on the north side of Taunton on 27th November 1949. The house was long and narrow, with rooms backing onto one another. The front room was used for special days, and a living room where we had the fireplace. There was a steep step into the dining room, and another step into the small kitchen. A bathroom had been added to the kitchen, which led to the outside white-washed toilet. It wasn't somewhere you lingered in the winter.

Both my parents were country people. My father, Len, had lived in Creech St. Michael near the canal. His local village school held swimming lessons in the canal. They owned an orchard with pigs and made cider with the apples. As was the custom then, my father left school at fourteen and joined his father to work for the Great Western Railways. He undertook a five-year apprenticeship as a carpenter.

My mother, Frances, lived with her three sisters in Rose Cottage in North Curry along with their mother. The girls lost their father when Frances was three. My mother worked as a secretary for a brewery company in Taunton. They both cycled from the countryside into Taunton every day for work.

Towards the end of our photo album there are photos of us as a family in Lossiemouth when I was four. We stayed with friends my father had made while stationed with the RAF during the war. My father said that our mother made us pack-up and come home early. There was a polio epidemic in the next village. Polio was still a deadly virus.

In early September 1955, when I was five, we went on holiday and stayed in a caravan at Blue Anchor. Blue Anchor is not far from Minehead. Even now there is no village, nor are there any shops. It's an area of beach and countryside. In the evenings the only sound is of the sea when the tide is in. Steam trains regularly puff their way along the coast and stop at Blue Anchor station.

It's almost as if, for my family, time stopped after that sunny September day.

We played on the beach and splashed in the waves; I loved to paddle at any opportunity. We didn't know at the time, but we were about to experience a random, unpredictable blow that would have an irreversible impact on us all.

CHAPTER 2

A Young Life
Paralysed

It was September 1955. Stuart was nine and I was five years old. We were having a birthday party to celebrate both my mother and father's birthday.

I started to feel ill. I felt hot and feverish with a headache and I ached all over. I cried as my father walked to the local phone booth down the road and called the doctor.

The doctor arrived and examined me. He said that I had all the symptoms of the deadly polio virus. An ambulance sped around the corner, sirens blaring and lights flashing. In the short space of time it took for the ambulance to arrive, I had become completely paralysed and lay limp on the bed. One of the ambulance men I spoke to later said I was like a rag doll. They rushed me to the isolation hospital in Cheddon Road. Polio is highly contagious.

My family was stunned at this awful news. At the time there was no vaccination to prevent polio and there were regular outbreaks around the country. Within an hour my mother was experiencing the same symptoms. My father ran once more to the local phone booth. Within an hour another ambulance raced along our street and took my mother to the same Isolation Hospital.

It all happened so quickly.

My father wanted to go with the ambulance but he needed to stay at home with Stuart. They were scared as they waited to see if either of them was going to experience any polio symptoms. A few hours earlier we had all been a happy family having fun and now we were split up in the most terrible way.

Stuart was upset at seeing his mother and sister being taken away so quickly and asked to share my father's bed for the night. When Stuart woke up the next morning, he couldn't move his legs. The polio virus had hit again. My father felt numb as he phoned for another ambulance. They both entered the Isolation Hospital.

My father hadn't shown any signs of contracting polio but he was put into isolation just to make sure. My family was now totally split up and unable to see or comfort each other. After a few days he was cleared and released, the only member of the family to have escaped catching polio.

I'd been taken to the hospital on my own. Where was my mother? Where was my father? Why weren't they with me? I wanted them to put their arms around me and tell me everything was alright. I needed them. They were at home when I left them. I called for them, shouted for them, but they couldn't hear me.

They didn't come.

I lay limp on the hospital bed in the small room. Nurses and doctors moved around me in white gowns and with masks on their faces. I couldn't move anything, I was completely paralysed. I could just about turn my head.

The nurses said that I needed to be quiet. They didn't explain what was happening to our family. I felt abandoned and alone. I wanted my mother. Between sobs, I shouted for her again and again, but she never came. I shouted for my father – surely he would come.

No-one came.

I cried and the tears rolled down my cheeks. I didn't know that my mother was next door struggling for her life. My mother was totally paralysed and the virus had also affected her lungs so that she had problems trying to breathe. She was deteriorating rapidly. She needed to be put in an iron lung which would breathe for her.

My mother was transferred by ambulance and police escort along the narrow A38 to Ham Green Hospital on the outskirts of Bristol, which had a section for people with infectious diseases. There were no available iron lungs, and so an iron lung was flown over from Sweden for my mother to use. She continued to fight for her life.

Now our family was even further apart.

My father wasn't allowed into either Stuart's room or my room. He could only look through the small window and wave to us. He was distraught at what was happening. I didn't understand what was happening to me, I was so distressed. I wanted things to be as they were; I wanted to go home.

At home, the Council acted quickly. Because polio was so contagious, the neighbours were scared. There was a possibility they could catch it as well. Men turned up wearing white suits and masks. They painted a large white cross on the front door. They barricaded the pavement and the road to prevent the public getting near. In the house, they took clothes, toys and anything we might have touched and burnt them. The whole house was fumigated. The property was then locked and bolted, with the key in possession of the authorities, with large warning posters telling everyone to stay clear. The newspapers reported that my father had pinned a notice to our gate, saying: *Nothing To Be Left Here Until Further Notice*, written in red pencil; and that he was going into voluntary exile. I'm not sure that my father did write that, I believe he would've left everything for the Council to do. He was far too distraught and busy visiting his family, in our separate hospitals, to have been involved.

Everyone was scared of contracting the polio virus as the effects are so devastating. It would be another three years before an effective vaccination was available and the spread of polio was halted. We learned that, after many pitfalls, there were two separate vaccinations created in the U.S.A., both of which helped eradicate the virus across the world.

My father was told he could go home. He looked at the big white cross as he unlocked the door. It wasn't as he'd left it. It looked bare of the things which had made it a home. Everything had changed so quickly. A few days before, we had been a happy family enjoying a party and now the silence in the house echoed. He had two children in hospital and his wife was in Bristol fighting for her life.

My father felt totally alone. Neighbours wanted to help him and console him but they daren't come near. There were no phones in those days other than the telephone booth down the road. There was no-one to speak to. He just wandered aimlessly with no real interest of where he was.

Then, as soon as it was safe, my mother's sister, Gladys, her husband Ivor and daughter Anne (13 at the time) moved temporarily from North Curry to our home so that they could look after my father while he tried to cope. He spent most of his days at the hospital.

Polio enters your body orally and infects the intestinal lining; it goes straight to the bloodstream and into the central nervous system and attacks the nerve cells in the spine. It depends on what part of the spinal column is attacked as to which nerves are affected. Some nerves are killed forever, other nerves are weakened. The only improvement is to try and work on the functioning and damaged nerves to take over.

I lay on the bed watching the nurses and doctors at work. I cried less and had stopped calling out. My mother and father hadn't heard me, they weren't coming. The doctors prodded my body to see if I could move my legs or arms. I was still completely paralysed. After three weeks they said I wasn't infectious anymore. My father came into the room. I begged him to take me home, but he couldn't.

The doctors told my father that we had probably contracted polio while on holiday in Blue Anchor, as it is a waterborne virus. The sewage was pumped directly into the sea in that area at that time. This they thought was the source of contamination. We had spent time playing in the sea. It was the only explanation they could give. My father hadn't gone into the sea.

I was transferred to a hospital with an orthopaedic ward to start my rehabilitation. Taunton hospital didn't have such a ward at that time, and so I was transported by ambulance to the Bath and Wessex Orthopaedic Hospital just outside of Bath.

Our father tried to see all of us every day. He rose at 2.00 a.m. to catch the early steam train to Bristol. He walked to the hospital to spend a few precious hours with my mother.

He sat by my mother, not knowing what to say. He talked of how well Stuart and I were doing. My mother was weak, her condition hadn't improved and she still relied on the iron lung for breathing. She had to listen to the plight our family was suffering but couldn't help us.

The iron lung was a large piece of medical equipment which required the patient to be entirely encased, apart from the head. The chamber was completely sealed and airtight. The machine breathed for the patient by means of pumps which increased and decreased the air pressure to work the lungs. My mother had a pipe inserted in her nose to allow air to flow into her lungs. My mother was face-upwards towards the ceiling. There was a mirror angled so that she could see the room. She was unable to say very much but desperately wanted to be with her family.

My father walked back to Bristol Station to catch another steam train to Bath. He walked to the hospital to visit me for a few hours. I was so bewildered by everything happening to me. Early afternoon, my father walked back to Bath Station to catch the train to Bristol and then back to Taunton to visit Stuart.

My father travelled to the three different hospitals for three weeks with barely any sleep, no nourishing meals, and his health began to suffer. Boils appeared on his legs and he could barely walk. A consultant saw him wobbling and looked at my father's legs. He wrote a prescription for Glycerine and Epsom Salts and said he had to rest more. The Great Western Railway were giving him time off but without pay.

A few weeks later, Stuart came to the same hospital as me but he was put in the Boys' Ward. His legs and lower back had been affected by the polio virus and were weak. I didn't realise he was so close, in the next ward to me. We never met. With no money coming in, my father was broke and he had to return to work.

On 11th November my father was out working when he received a message asking him to report to the railway office as soon as possible. They were sorry to have to tell him that his wife, our mother, had lost her fight to live and had died. It is hard to imagine how he felt.

Our family life was over. My father was now a widower, left with not only two young children to care for, but two disabled children in hospital with an uncertain future ahead and no mother to care for them.

CHAPTER 3

THE CHILDREN'S WARD

I was lifted out of the ambulance, put on a trolley and wheeled to the Children's Ward. One of the nurses pointed to an empty bed. I was transferred to that bed and the ambulance men disappeared from view.

Everything felt so strange and I didn't know where I was. I had travelled on my own in the back of the ambulance with no-one to comfort me. I badly needed my mother to be with me and reassure me but knew now that she wouldn't come. No-one had explained anything to me. I wore a hospital nightdress and was wrapped in a blanket. I had no possessions with me, no wash bag, comb or even a toy.

I wanted to move. Why couldn't I move? As hard as I tried, it was all I could do to move my head slightly to one side. I had come from a small room on my own to a huge ward full of children. After a while, the ward sister came over to me. She said 'You must be Rita'. I just looked at her. She introduced herself as Sister Mumford and gave me a warm smile. She wore a royal blue uniform with a white apron and starched white hat. She looked around for my belongings. I had none. She looked around to see if there was anyone with me. There was no-one.

The children's ward consisted of one big ward with two rows of old fashioned metal beds for thirty children. The children were aged between five and ten years old. It was a mixed ward and many of the children were long-stay patients. There were other children in the ward who'd been paralysed by polio.

The first few weeks went by in a haze. Doctors came to examine me and assess how much I could move. I could hear other children chatting but I couldn't see them. I wanted to join in but I felt too weak.

I gradually became accustomed to the hospital routine. With thirty children to get washed, fed, and beds made before the doctors and physiotherapists started to appear, it was a tight regime. The nurses wore pale blue starched uniforms complete with starched white hats. In the mornings, the nurses worked in pairs. The first two nurses entered the ward with a trolley of bowls and jugs of hot water to wash us. The next two nurses entered with a trolley of nighties and pyjamas and clean sheets.

The procedure was undertaken with precision. Nightdress removed, and I was washed with luke-warm water. A clean nightdress was grabbed off the trolley and put on me. The size varied every day, some too big or too small, but stretched to fit if necessary. I was rolled first one way whilst a nurse rolled a clean sheet towards me, and then I was rolled the other way while the other nurse took away the old sheet and pulled the clean sheet tight. The top bedclothes were tucked in a precise way at the corners and the two nurses worked quickly together.

A nurse took a comb out of her pocket to comb my hair. It wasn't easy to comb as I lay on my back. My hair soon got tangled and it hurt to have it combed. After a quick tug, they went to the next child. There were no mirrors so I never saw what I looked like. When the procedure was finished, the Sister marched into the ward to inspect their work. Everything had to be immaculate. I could hear the nurses saying 'Yes Sister, no Sister' as they rushed around correcting anything, however small.

We were expected to wait for bedpan rounds, usually after each meal. The nurses appeared with large trolleys stacked with bedpans. With quick precision, the nurses either told us to lift ourselves up if we could, or they would lift us up onto the bedpan. We were all put on the bedpans at the same time with no curtains for privacy. We just had to wait for the nurses to come around again to lift us off them.

Matron was in charge of all the nursing staff throughout the hospital. She would suddenly appear in the ward as if by magic, wrapped in her dark blue cloak. She was of slender build with white hair. She stood by the entrance of the ward looking around at us all. She commanded complete hush just by her presence.

Occasionally Matron walked around the ward. When she asked if we were well, we replied 'Yes, Matron'. Then, with a swish of her cloak, she disappeared. After that, we could relax and start to play again. She was strict but I noticed a twinkle in her eye as if we were her family. She reminded me of an elderly grandmother.

The whole hospital was built on one level in a U-shape. At one end was a huge physiotherapist department and theatre. At the other end, an occupational department and plaster room with wards in between. A corridor ran the full length.

The hospital (now a car park, as the hospital has been demolished) had originally been built for people with tuberculosis but when the need diminished, it had become a general orthopaedic hospital. The outside section of the wards was made entirely of glass doors which could be pushed back in a concertina style for fresh air, to aid recovery. The ward walls and floor were made of dark polished wooden panels.

A hospital in the 1950s was very basic. There were no curtains to pull around the beds for privacy. We had no button to press for help. If we needed a nurse we had to shout. There was no television or radio. I never saw a bath or a shower, we all had bed baths. We ate and drank from tin plates and mugs. We always had a cooked breakfast but it was usually burnt and cold and looked disgusting, as did most of the meals. There was no choice.

The hospital doors were kept locked, except for restricted visiting times. My father came to visit me when he could, but my life had changed so much, everything seemed to be a blur. After a few weeks my father had to come and explain that my mother had died. I don't think it registered; I had already stopped calling for her. Family life was fading as the months went by. I was no longer in a family environment.

CHAPTER 4

In Solitary

I was so frustrated at not being able to move and with no-one to comfort me, I often cried. One day, very early on, one of the nurses came over to the bed and told me to stop it. A small boy hobbled over to me on crutches. He looked around and whispered to me not to cry, and quickly disappeared.

Suddenly, two nurses burst through the doors of the ward and grabbed each end of my bed. Without saying a word, they wheeled me in my bed out of the ward and along the corridor. They opened the doors of a small side ward which was just big enough for my bed, and pushed me and my bed into the small room. They said that when I'd stopped behaving so badly, I could come out. They shut the doors and walked away. I'd been put into solitary confinement for crying. It was their way of punishing me.

The nurses said that it upset the other children. I was five, unable to move, distressed, and lonely. The side room was just big enough for my bed. There were no windows, just white walls and double doors now closed. For a while I sobbed even more, but gradually stopped. I didn't want to be in there, and I was afraid of being forgotten.

After what seemed to be ages, a nurse appeared at the door and asked if I had stopped crying. I tried to nod, I was afraid of speaking in case I cried again. The nurse reminded me that every time I cried I'd be put in solitary confinement. I had to learn this rule quickly. The other children understood where I'd been, but said nothing. I often heard crying at night from under the bedclothes. It was a harsh lesson to learn at an early age.

Every day the porters lifted me onto a trolley, covered me with a grey hospital blanket and pushed me down to the physiotherapy room for exercises. They exercised my legs and arms trying to get the muscles to respond. I heard later that the first nine months are vital, as any weak muscles could be encouraged to strengthen. Little did I realise that I'd be in hospital for much longer than that. Even when I was ready, my father was informed that I couldn't go home with no mother to care for me.

The polio virus kills the nerves in the spinal column. All muscles respond to the nerves which tell the muscles what to do. If I want to lift my leg, the brain sends a message along the nerves to the appropriate muscles so that the muscles respond: and I lift my leg. If that nerve is dead, then no message reaches the muscles and there is no response. There may be a chance that the nerve isn't completely dead and might be encouraged to work. That's why exercise is so important.

Every day they repeated the same exercises. They stretched my fingers trying to get them to move. They threw me small beanbags to encourage me to catch them. They moved my legs in and out, bending them, and rotated my ankles.

After several weeks of exercising, I started to move my fingers. They propped me up and held my arms out to help me catch the beanbags. As the weeks went by my arms began, gradually, to respond. They did the same to my legs. They moved my feet up and down, moved my legs in bicycle motion, but they didn't respond.

My back was very weak and I couldn't sit up without falling over or sliding down into the bed. The nurses were instructed to roll me onto my front and to push a thick wedge down the front of me to prop me up. At first, I just flopped onto the front of the bed, but my curiosity to see what was happening in the ward made me want to lift up my head. Every day I tried to lift my head to see the other children in the ward. Gradually I learnt to prop my head up, with my arms and elbows on the bed.

My bed was turned around so that I was facing into the ward and I could look through the bars at the head of my bed to see the other children in the ward. This became my usual position. I had a metal U-shaped cradle to lift the bedclothes off my feet to stop them being squashed, with a pillow under my feet to support them. My elbows were constantly sore from leaning on them and after a wash the nurses applied cream. As I looked into the ward I could chat to the other children. Many of them were also lying on their front.

I still had no personal belongings and my locker remained empty. The hospital supplied everything for most long-stay children. My father was struggling to cope. He was just glad that the hospital could supply what I needed. The clothes were often faded but were clean.

Each day a nurse patrolled the ward with a book and enquired whether we had been to the toilet properly. They seemed to know if we lied. I so wanted them to just tick the book and move on.

Twice a week a nurse came around and gave us a spoonful of syrup of figs; and with the same kind of frequency, Sister marched into the ward and looked around as though trying to decide who to pick. We kept very still and held our breath; we knew what this meant. She picked three children by name and disappeared. Nurses appeared and pushed the beds with those children into the treatment room which was big enough for three beds. It was their turn to have an enema.

One day the finger was pointed at me and they pushed me into the treatment room. A nurse rolled me onto one side and inserted a thick brown tube into my bottom. Then they held the tube up high with a funnel on top and poured warm soapy water into my bottom. I kept as quiet as I could. I knew there would be trouble if I cried. Anyway, I was getting braver. You never heard the other children cry. The tube was removed and I had to wait a while before they came with a bedpan. The whole procedure was extremely painful and stressful.

I felt part of the ward now. I knew most of the children. I could take part in some of the games, even from lying on my front. I was one of the youngest and looked up to the older children to learn how to fit in and survive. Some of the children got up during the day and used crutches or a wheelchair to move around. They passed around what toys might be available.

The head of my family was now Sister Mumford, and the children were my new brothers and sisters. Although Stuart was so close in the next ward, I never saw him and I had already begun to forget him.

CHAPTER 5

VISITING TIMES

There was only one public entrance into the hospital. This was through a heavy wooden door, kept locked at all times except for visiting hours. Anyone visiting had to wait outside the door in all kinds of weather until the door was unlocked. There was no covered area or any refreshments available. Most parents, like my father, had travelled many miles to come to the hospital. There was no café within or outside the hospital. At 2.00 p.m. precisely a porter opened the door to allow relatives and visitors to enter.

The hospital staff saw parents and visitors as a nuisance. They said that parents upset a child and hindered their recovery. The staff had a job to do and visiting times stopped them. So very different from today. The Sister was quite harsh with parents who might question anything about their child. Parents were requested to sit on the allocated seats by the bed and not touch the bed.

Visiting times were every Tuesday and Thursday afternoon between 2.00 and 4.00 p.m., and some evenings. At the weekend there was visiting every Saturday afternoon and one Sunday a month from 2.00 and 4.00 p.m. The

Great Western Railway had agreed to allow my father every Tuesday so that he could visit my brother and me. We didn't have a car and my father couldn't drive, so he had to rely on steam trains for travelling to Bath and visit us. In the 1950s travelling by steam train was slow and unpredictable. He caught the train from Taunton to Bristol and changed for Bath. The trains were often delayed. He then walked to the hospital. The long journey sometimes made him late for visiting time but the Sister still told him to leave at 4.00 p.m. for the long journey back.

Most parents visited their child for two full hours. My father needed to visit both Stuart and me within the 2-hour slot so we had less time with him. I only saw my father for one hour a week. It wasn't long enough to mean anything. I never knew when it was Tuesday, I had lost all sense of dates and times. He suddenly appeared, chatted for a while, and disappeared. I soon forgot him afterwards and continued playing with the other children.

At 4.00 p.m. the Sister marched around the ward, ringing a large bell, ushering the visitors out. This was performed in a quick and regimented manner. A porter waited by the open door to marshal visitors out, and then he shut and bolted the door again. We were locked in, and my father was locked out.

One Tuesday, my father came to the hospital with his own father, my grandfather. The train was delayed and they raced to the hospital to try and get in before the end of visiting time. A porter apprehended them at the door. 'Too late,' he said. The visitors were about to leave, so the door was shut in their faces. They had come all that way for nothing. I never did see my grandfather again, he was killed during work not long after.

The hospital was now my home. The Sister and nurses were my family. My father was someone who came to say hello and disappeared again. He was struggling to cope, with no-one to help him; it was hard for us all. He told me that he never missed a Tuesday. He hoped with all his heart that one day Stuart and I could eventually come home.

My aunts occasionally came to see me at weekends and sometimes they brought my cousins. We had been a close family and I was always pleased to see them. Travelling the 120-mile return journey in the 1950s was never easy. They sent me postcards when they were unable to come.

There was no hairdresser facility in the hospital; it was up to the relatives to sort this out if their child was in the hospital for any length of time. Aunt Gladys arrived one day and saw the state of my matted hair. She demanded a pair of scissors from the nurse to cut my hair. I started to scream in the hope that she would stop. She said 'Enough of that, my girl,' and continued to cut off my hair. I have no idea what it looked like as I had no mirror, but it was no longer matted.

There were no hankies or tissues supplied for us to use, we just used our sleeves if needed. There was no-one to cut our fingernails, we had to get used to biting them.

Some children never had any visitors. The parents of other children tried to include them. I remember one young girl asked my father if he could be her father as well.

Every time my father came I asked for a doll, a doll I could cuddle but he never brought one. All my toys had been burnt at home. He often told me that he tried, but the shops were always shut when he had any spare time.

One day, Sister Mumford surprised me. She came up to my bed and gave me a handmade, felt, standing rabbit, fully clothed; I thought, straight from Alice in Wonderland. She said 'I know you want a doll. I don't have a doll, but I have a rabbit.' I smiled and hugged the rabbit. I had something to hold. Under all that outward severity there was a Sister who cared. She smiled back at me and left the ward.

CHAPTER 6

HOSPITAL LIFE

I couldn't read or write. Before I caught polio I had attended North Town Primary School, but as the months went by I soon forgot everything. There were other children in the same situation. For a few hours every day a school mistress provided lessons to the thirty children in the ward who were aged between five and ten.

Our ward was long. If the tutor stood at the far end, we couldn't see or hear her. All of the children did the same lesson regardless of age. You either understood the lesson or you didn't. She handed out well-worn books. Many of them already had the answers written in them for those who could read or add up.

I was rarely at school, as every day I was wheeled to the physiotherapy room for exercises. Getting me mobile was more important. There was no time to give us individual lessons and there were never any children's books in the ward. If I was in the ward during the school sessions, the teacher gave me crayons and paper and suggested what I should draw. To begin with, I found this hard as I couldn't make my hands hold a crayon, and if I did I couldn't put enough pressure on it to draw.

Gradually, I started drawing.

One day, the teacher asked me to draw my house. I tried to think what my house looked like. It was all a blur so I just drew what I thought a house looked like. I had coloured the roof purple. The teacher picked up my drawing and showed the other children, pointing out that there are no houses with purple roofs. She told me that I should have known better.

At physiotherapy, they constantly moved my limbs and encouraged me to move. I could now hold my head up and move my arms a bit, but they soon got tired. There was still no movement in my legs. I couldn't sit up without help or stay sitting up because of my lack of balance. However, I was beginning to do more for myself, and I could catch and throw a ball short distances. As my hands and arms began to move I could play more with the other children.

Thirty children in a ward can become noisy and the Sister would often march into the ward and shout 'Silence!' We immediately became silent. If we tried to whisper or talk the punishment would be solitary confinement. When Sister marched out we stayed silent for a while, but it wasn't long before we were chatting again.

Along one side of the ward there were those concertina-style folding glass doors which opened onto a raised veranda, overlooking a large lawn. They were my only window onto the world at that time. The glass doors were opened every day unless it was raining, even on the coldest day. On a good day we were wheeled outside in our beds onto the veranda. It was nice to be in the sun, but if there was a cold wind we huddled under the bedclothes. To begin with, I tried to wait until I was the last person to be pushed in my bed onto the veranda, to get more protection from the wind.

This was a big mistake. My bed was then under the eaves of the ward and earwigs fell onto the bed and scuttled away. I hated them and constantly looked to see where they landed next. The nurses were too busy to take any notice. After that, I decided I would rather be out first and cope with the weather than share my bed with earwigs. In the evening we could hear cockroaches scurrying along the floor.

One day a porter arrived with a trolley, wrapped me in a blanket and pushed me out to a waiting ambulance packed with other patients. I arrived at the old part of the Roman baths to have warm water therapy sessions in one of the smaller baths. We were wheeled along lengthy, narrow corridors into a small room with just enough room for two high, narrow beds. I was scared to move in case I fell off the bed. A nurse came to help me change into a swimming costume they provided, and I was carried through the door to the waiting therapist in the pool.

I lay on my back with the therapist's hands holding my body. She moved me through the warm thermal water and coaxed me to try various exercises. I felt light and it was easier to move my body. I was lifted out and wrapped in really hot towels which felt wonderful although the heat soon dispersed. I returned to the room, where the nurse helped me get dressed.

One afternoon I arrived at the baths to discover I had been put in a room on my own, the other bed stayed empty. I was used to being in a room with someone else. The whole place scared me because it was so big and old, everything echoed as the trolleys and wheelchairs were pushed along the corridor. I only felt at ease when I was with someone. After my swimming session I told the nurse that I didn't want to be left on my own. 'Don't be silly,' she said, and left me.

I was wrapped in a blanket and I had to wait for the ambulance men to come and pick me up. I could hear the trolleys and wheelchairs trundling back and forth as well as the cheerful whistle of one of the ambulance men. I told myself that I would be next.

I heard a heavy door slam shut in the distance, echoing along the corridor. It became really quiet. No noise from the trolleys or wheelchairs and no voices. I was convinced I'd been left behind. I looked down at the floor, but the bed was so high there was no way I could get off or go anywhere. I was so scared. After what seemed like ages, an ambulance man suddenly appeared. I cried out that I had been left behind. The ambulance man told me not to be so stupid. There were other people to load besides myself and I would have to learn to wait. I knew they had forgotten me, but couldn't argue. No-one was going to believe me. Everyone was very subdued as the ambulance travelled back to hospital.

CHAPTER 7

CHRISTMAS IN HOSPITAL

November arrived and it was bonfire night. We were going to have a bonfire and a firework display in the grounds of the hospital. We were so excited. In the evening we were wheeled in our beds onto the veranda. I was lying on my front as usual and we were each given a candle to hold in a small container, and a sparkler. A porter handed out bags of chips to each of us. They were lovely. I said to the nurse standing beside me that I was going to keep them hot by holding them over the candle, but I soon ate them. That was such a special treat.

We shouted and clapped as the fireworks shone in the night. The bonfire seemed huge and lit up the whole area around us. All the people from the other wards were outside like us. The excitement of the sparklers and the fireworks made this a night to remember, and it was ages before the nurses could get us settled down for the night. I heard later that it had been organised by the Scouts.

Stuart had his tenth birthday on 1st November, and I had my sixth birthday on 27th November. An article was printed in the Somerset County Gazette telling everyone how we had caught polio and were celebrating our birthdays in the hospital in Bath. There was a photo printed with the article showing my mother, Stuart and me looking fit and well at the top of Burrow Mump which is situated on the Somerset Levels.

Everyone was talking about Christmas. The department store Evans and Owens in Bath invited all the children to the toy store to choose a toy for Christmas. I was wrapped up in blankets and laid on a stretcher for the ambulance journey. Then two nurses carried me around so that I could look at the toys and make my choice. My excitement turned to frustration at seeing so many toys I couldn't use so I said that I didn't want anything.

In the end, I came back to the hospital holding a tube of blow bubble. The next day the nurses rolled me over and propped me up and I asked for the tube of blow bubble. They gave it to me along with a teddy bear which had been sent to me from the children of North Town School, the school I had originally attended. Each child had brought a penny to school which they used to buy me a teddy bear. I couldn't unscrew the lid of the blow bubble so the nurse did this. She placed the tube on the bed and the handle in my hand. I dipped the end in and as I pulled it out the tub tipped over and all the solution ran out onto my bed, and spread onto my teddy bear. I wasn't popular, and that was the end of my blow bubble present.

My father was really pleased to hear about the visit to the toy shop, as Christmas was going to be a hard enough time for him. He was eager to hear what I had bought, but I had nothing to show him except that my teddy now had curly hair.

I was going to spend my first Christmas away from home. My brother Stuart was going to spend Christmas in the next ward to me, but still we hadn't met. A brother and sister so near to one another and yet separated. I wonder why no-one thought to help us meet. We were so like strangers to each other when we eventually met again.

My father was going to spend Christmas without us. There were no trains on Christmas Day. It must've been a very lonely time for him.

On Christmas Day I awoke to find that Father Christmas had been and there was a stocking at the end of my bed. With great excitement, I opened my present. Father Christmas had given me a fabric toy elephant. The elephant stood upright on two legs with puffed-up satin turquoise trousers. I decided to call him Jumbo and he joined the rabbit that Sister Mumford had given me, as well as my teddy bear.

Later on, Father Christmas appeared in person to our great excitement and handed out more presents. As I opened mine, I realised with dismay that it was another elephant exactly like the first. I couldn't understand why Father Christmas hadn't remembered that he'd already given me one, and I started to complain. A passing nurse said she was sure she could find a good home for the elephant if I didn't want it. I clung to him and called him Mumbo.

Mumbo and Jumbo became very popular. The elephants were soon passed around the ward like most of the toys. I never thought of anything as being just mine, the children in the ward shared everything. The elephants were often thrown from bed to bed, and more than once a nurse would take one home to repair. One of the elephants got stuck on a rafter beam across the ceiling and a porter had to come with a ladder to get him down. Gradually, the elephants wore out and disappeared.

In the New Year a human circus came to entertain us. Clowns and jugglers made us laugh, performing various tricks around the ward. All of a sudden a man approached me holding what I thought was a snake. I panicked and started screaming. The nurses tried to re-assure me that it was the man's arm painted to look like a snake. To me it was very real and I feared it was going to bite me. The nurses grabbed my bed and quickly pushed me out of the ward and into the side room, closing the door on me. I was scared, but there were no comforting words, just solitary confinement again. I had to be punished for making a scene. I stayed there for a long time. When I returned to the ward, the circus had gone and everything was back to normal.

Spring arrived, and I could sit up for a while leaning against a backrest, but spent most of the time on my front. I had become very good at managing like this, although my elbows were always very sore from leaning on them. I could now eat on my front, wash my hands in a bowl, and play. I had to peer through the iron bars of my headboard to see the other children, but I was used to that.

I hated the hospital food. We were often punished with some form of solitary confinement if we didn't eat our food. There was always someone mobile, either on crutches or in a wheelchair, willing to pass food around out of sight of the nurses to avoid detection. I got quite good at throwing marmite sandwiches, which I hated at the time, and anything else that could be thrown. I remember one girl falling out of bed in her attempt to catch whatever I had thrown. There was a great hush as the nurse asked for an explanation as to why she had fallen out of bed. The girl said she didn't know, it just happened! The rest of us kept very quiet.

One evening I wasn't so lucky. Supper was poached egg on a solid sticky mass of very dark soggy spinach. One look and I wanted to heave. The nurse stood over me to watch me eat. I just looked at it with my mouth firmly shut. The nurse sighed and took the plate away. I thought it was all over, but a few minutes later two nurses appeared.

They grabbed my bed and pushed me out of the ward. I thought they were going to put me in the side room again, but they turned in the opposite direction. It was dark in the corridor and I stayed quiet as they pushed me along. They opened the double doors into the large physiotherapy room. They then slammed the doors shut behind them and walked away. My punishment was to be left in that large, very dark physiotherapy room on my own for the night. I was six years old.

In the dark, the physiotherapy room looked so different, with all the equipment throwing weird shapes against the wall. Dark shapes seem to leap at me. With eyes wide open, I studied each shape, expecting it to move. When I looked at another shape, I swear the previous shape moved and my eyes darted back to look at that shape again. I was too scared to sleep, though at some point I must've dozed.

Early the next morning two nurses came and pushed me back to the ward. They didn't speak to me and I stayed very quiet. The other children wanted me to tell them where I'd spent the night but I just shook my head. I didn't want to talk about it. Even now, I feel sick whenever I see spinach.

I learnt about our resident ghost 'Flannel Foot'. Other children said he had been a patient in the hospital and had died on the operating table. The story was that nurses had wrapped his feet in large pieces of sheeting called 'flannels' to stop the blood, but he'd still died. It was said that he roamed the wards at night when there was a 3 in the date, touching every third bed. We spent ages trying to calculate which bed he might touch, because whichever side of the ward he started meant he would touch a different bed.

Suddenly, someone announced that it was a date with a 3 in it. We all looked at each other with apprehension as we wondered if we might see the ghost that night. Most of us were slightly scared and we all became quiet as the night came. We promised to stay awake to see him, but we were usually fast asleep soon after the lights went off. Sometimes, in the dark, we heard an unusual noise in the corridor and would say 'Flannel Foot!' Of course, we never saw the ghost.

The hospital provided hot water bottles. They were round and made of pottery but they were being replaced with modern rubber hot water bottles. As I was now one of the longest-staying patients, I was allowed one of the new type bottles. The rubber hot water bottle was red and there was a raised picture of a pig on the front.

I asked the nurse if I could borrow her scissors. At wash time, I emptied the hot water bottle and cut out the pig on the front. I proudly showed my efforts to the nurse and asked if I could keep the red pig. The nurse grabbed the scissors and the hot water bottle and marched out of the ward.

I had to be punished. The children were going on stretchers in ambulances to the Zoo but I was told that I had to remain behind. Nurses got out a bag of clothes and helped the children get dressed in hospital day clothes. I watched while all the children were wrapped in blankets and carried out to the ambulances on trolleys. Everyone was excited except me. Soon the ward was quiet and empty. The nurses left me alone and no-one spoke to me. I was angry and ignored their excited faces when the children returned.

Stuart went home in June, but I didn't miss him as, of course, we never saw one another. He'd also been to the gym every day for exercises and became more mobile. He now wore a half-calliper on one leg and a spinal support to keep his back straight, as his spine was weak.

Soon after this, we had another outing, this time to the beach, and I could go. The nurses found me a dress and cardigan and wrapped me in a blanket. We were packed tightly in an ambulance and on our way. The windows of the ambulance were dark so it was difficult to look out.

My father and Stuart had travelled by train, and met me as I got out of the ambulance. There was a lady with my father who was keen to meet me. They carried me down to the sand and we all sat together while I played in the sand. We ate sandwiches for lunch. It was the longest time I'd spent with my father and Stuart for ages. Other family members had joined their children. It was such a good day.

As I waved goodbye to my father, Stuart, the new lady and I think her parents, it didn't occur to me that maybe I should be going home with them. I knew they were going home and I was going to mine. My home was my ward and they lived in a house somewhere. I'd accepted that we lived apart.

CHAPTER 8

GETTING MOBILE

A nurse brought me a wheelchair to try. It was a big, old fashioned, heavy metal wheelchair, and meant for an adult. The nurse wrapped me in a blanket and lifted me into the wheelchair, pushing me to the table for dinner. The wheelchair supported me and helped me to sit up. It was so nice to be out of bed and not have to look at other children through the bars of the bed. It'd been like looking through the bars of a cage.

I wanted to move around the ward but the wheelchair was so big. I soon found that if I leant to one side I could reach one wheel to move it, then I did the same on the other wheel. In time, I learned how to propel myself around the ward. It felt wonderful to be mobile again. It also helped to build up the muscles in my arms.

Each day I was able to spend longer in the wheelchair. I visited the children in their beds to play with them. Dinnertime was the only meal we were allowed to sit at the table. The wheelchair gave me more freedom.

I had become friends with a girl called Pauline. She couldn't remember how long she'd been in hospital and had no recollection of living anywhere else. I never saw any family or relatives visit her. I think Pauline spent her entire life in hospital. Every time I went into hospital, Pauline was always there in the ward and I was always pleased to see her.

The porters now took me to the physiotherapist department in a wheelchair. We laughed and joked on the way. I knew all the porters. Now I was sitting up I could look around me as we made our way to the physiotherapy.

As I didn't have many visitors, a volunteer came to read to me. I didn't have to share her with anyone else. She knew I couldn't read but showed me the pictures in the books as she turned the pages. We didn't get much individual attention, there were so many of us in the ward, so I relished the time she spent with me.

The Duke of Edinburgh was visiting Bath. We were all wrapped in blankets, and put on stretchers and taken by ambulance to the city centre. There we lined the street and waited to see him go by in a car. Our stretchers were laid on boards all in a row. We were each given a flag to wave and the nurses stood smartly behind us. I hadn't been outside of the hospital for such a long time. I was mesmerised by everything around me. The shops, the number of people, the traffic! Where had they all come from? I waved my flag as the royal procession went by. We had no television so never had anything to remind us of what life was like outside.

I could do more and was eager to try different things. One morning the sun was shining and I decided to do some baking. I didn't have any ingredients and wondered what I could use instead. I must've helped my mother bake cakes to have this idea. Each child was given an old squash bottle of water to keep on their locker, and the water was renewed every day. I decided the bottle lids would make super cake cases. I pushed myself around the ward, removing the lids and put them up on a tray. I poured a drop of orange squash into each cake case. Then I shook in some talcum powder because it resembled flour and added a dash of water. I gave each case a good stir and carried them out, on my lap, to cook in the sun on a wall.

Later that morning, the cleaning ladies came to refill the bottles and enquired where all the lids had gone. I told them they could have the lids back once my cakes had finished cooking in the sun. They were not amused as they disappeared with the tray of lids to clean before replacing on the bottles. Fortunately, they didn't tell on me, so I avoided punishment this time.

I didn't have any clothes of my own and relied on the nighties and dresses the hospital supplied. This was probably the case with many of the children in the ward. With only my father to look after this side of things, it wasn't a high priority as he struggled with daily life. He was now trying to look after my brother at home while working and coming to visit me.

On one of my father's visits, the Sister told him that as I was now more mobile he needed to buy me some knickers. My father had no idea what he really needed to buy, and looked around the shops in Bath on his next visit. He found a shop, and explained what he needed. He didn't know what size I was, but said I was six years old.

The assistant held up a lacy pair of knickers, commenting how nice they were. My father bought them and brought them to the hospital. The Sister explained that they weren't very practical and also I would need more than one pair. The next time he visited, my father had to return the lacy knickers and bought some plain cotton ones.

The aim was to get me up and walking again. I could never do this on my own, as my legs lay limp on the bed. No exercises could get them to move. I was pushed on my bed to the Appliance Centre. Someone took measurements of my legs and made a calliper for each leg. The calliper consisted of a rod of iron each side of my legs with metal supports covered in leather to keep my legs in place. They made a ring of iron around the top of each calliper also covered in padding and leather which fitted under my bottom and in the groin. The callipers had to be strong enough to hold me up so that I could stand. They were also very heavy.

I had a knee support which was a square of leather strapped into place to keep my knee straight. I had to go for endless fitting sessions to make sure the callipers were just right. The straps pinched as they were pulled tight and the metal ring dug into my groin. They had to make special shoes with holes at each side of the shoe so that the calliper could be fitted to the shoe. They were so uncomfortable. This doesn't happen now. People are taught how to be independent using a wheelchair. In the 1950s the solution was to get everyone up and walking again, however hard or painful it was.

Two physiotherapists lifted me off the bed to stand me up with my callipers on. They put me in a square frame on wheels with crutch supports to go under the arms to support me. I just hung there suspended by my arms. They asked me to try and stand up, but this seemed impossible. After a lot of effort I gradually learnt to stand, leaning heavily on the crutches. Now I had to try and move my legs, which seemed rooted to the floor. The heavy callipers made my legs feel like a lead weight.

The wheels moved but I couldn't make my legs follow them. The physiotherapist said that if I lifted my shoulder up and leant to one side, my leg would come off the ground. Then do the same to move the other leg. Over the weeks I could shuffle my legs forward. It was exhausting. After many weeks of constant practise I managed to take a few steps.

Every day I had to practise walking and did more exercises to strengthen my arms and back. Some of the strength had returned to my arms but I was never going to get all my strength back. I had to learn to use what strength I had.

With more practise I could walk short distances. As the summer progressed, my walking improved. My callipers didn't bend at the knee so I could only walk. I didn't know how to stand up or sit down. When I sat up to try and help put my callipers on, I just fell back down again because my back was still weak. There was still so much that I couldn't do. My consultant, Mr Hedley Hall, came to see how I was doing. I turned to him defiantly and said 'Look, I am walking! *You* said I would never walk again.'

I gradually learnt to walk with two walking sticks which replaced the walking frame. If I lifted my shoulder up too far my leg went too far and I did the splits landing on the floor. The physiotherapist tied a piece of string to the inside metal bar of each calliper to keep my legs a certain distance and no further. It was hard work trying to keep my balance and also willing my legs to move as I slowly moved forward.

I was by now a very different little girl from the child who'd entered hospital. I was a tough child and could hold my own in difficult circumstances. I'd learnt from older children how to behave to get the best results. I knew when and how to get attention and when to melt into the background if there was any punishment forthcoming. It didn't always work, but it helped me to survive. I was more likely to hit out or shout. If a nurse was looking to see who had done something wrong, I had learnt to stare them out. I was less likely to cry if I stared at them. They usually backed off first and would pick out someone else.

I never received any comfort or affection during my stay in hospital as a child. My father talked to me during visiting times, but found it hard to show any affection. It was also discouraged by the staff, who continued to say it could upset a child. I was becoming hardened to the way of life in the ward. I was still only 6 years old but I felt that I was in control. Even though I eventually went home, I don't think my father and I ever properly connected again.

CHAPTER 9

My Father
Someone New

My father worked for the Great Western Railways as a carpenter joiner. This involved him travelling widely by trains for repair jobs. In Spring 1956 he was working near East Huntspill. He'd met a local couple who asked him in for a hot drink when the weather was bad. The husband had a sister, Kathleen, who lived in London and came to visit regularly. The next time Kathleen came to visit they introduced her to my father.

My father was waiting for his train to get home and Kath was waiting for a train back to London. They sat in the waiting room and chatted. My father told her about both of us and how we were in hospital recovering from polio, and how he didn't know how he was going to get us home.

Kathleen worked for the Civil Service after leaving the Women's Royal Artillery, where she had worked during the war. Her fiancé had died as a result of the war. She offered to send us postcards in hospital to help cheer us up. So Stuart and myself started to receive these postcards. My father wrote to thank her and a correspondence began.

Stuart, who was now at home, had to get up at the same time as my father and go to a neighbour for breakfast prior to going to school. He returned to the neighbour's house after school and waited until my father returned from work. Then Stuart went home for dinner. My father wasn't used to cooking for himself and often just made do, but with Stuart at home he had to think about what to cook, with some interesting results.

Kath came down to stay with a neighbour in the summer and came with my father and my brother to visit me. I said a polite 'Hello' and thanked her for the postcards. She also brought me some flowers and a paper doll with different paper dresses that I could dress her in. They didn't last long, but I do remember playing with them.

One day my father visited me with Kath, and with Stuart too. I was in a wheelchair wrapped in a blanket. We had special permission to go for a stroll around the hospital grounds. There were large green lawns and beds of flowers. The hospital and grounds are now a car park.

Kath invited my father and Stuart to London to stay and they all got on well. They continued to correspond and meet up. I knew nothing of this at the time. Once visiting time was over my father, and anyone else, was forgotten. My father wanted me home but as he lived on his own and worked full-time, it couldn't happen because there was no-one to care for me at home. There was no help through Social Services in those days. Kath was thirty-five and had never married and lived at home with her parents. My father was also thirty-five. This new lady was keen to help my father get me home. There was a bond there that drew them together.

I had met Kath a few times now. I liked the postcards she sent and the gifts she bought me but didn't really understand what it all meant. The role of a mother and father was now alien to me. I think my father tried to tell me but I was always busy playing and didn't take in what he said. I had no idea this lady would become important to me.

If my father mentioned home, I looked puzzled. After so long in hospital, I couldn't remember home. I thought I would stay in the ward forever. I thought I *was* home.

My new mother-to-be was keen to start a new life and move out of London and live in Taunton. She had a new purpose in life, to get me out of hospital and bring us all together as a family again. They decided to get married at the end of the year and then it would be possible for me to come home.

CHAPTER 10

In Limbo

It was September 1956 and I was 6 years old. My father arrived at the ward to visit me. He looked around and couldn't find me. Someone said 'She's gone.' My father went to the Sister's office to ask where I was. I'd been transferred to the Orthopaedic Extension at Southstoke House, Midford Road, Combe Down, Bath. There had been no warning. No-one had let my father know. When he asked where I was, he was directed across a field of cabbages towards a large house.

The hospital had decided that there was nothing more they could do for me. I couldn't go home. I'd been sent to the extension unit to wait for a decision as to where I went next. I was in limbo.

I'd been playing in the ward when two porters arrived with a trolley. They put the scant contents of my locker into a black bag and then transferred me onto the trolley. I thought I was going to physio, so didn't query it. I was still in my nightdress as the nurses hadn't dressed me yet. The callipers were dumped on the trolley. I was out of the ward before I knew it, with no chance to say goodbye to anyone.

I arrived at a big house. I was carried in, along some corridors, and then I was carried upstairs. A nurse opened a door into a small room. I was carried in and put in a large cot with sides. Another person carried my callipers, pushed them under the bed, and then they departed.

The small room was completely silent. Four walls, with a door to my left and a window to my right. The window was high up and all I could see from my cot was a small patch of sky.

No-one had said anything to me. I had no idea where I was, or what was happening to me. On the ward I'd been able to see so much more and look through the glass doors. There'd been a lot going on around me. Here, there was nothing.

I sat for a long time in the quiet and dimly-lit room, waiting for something to happen. There were four cots in the room. They looked empty. As my eyes got used to the poor light I suddenly realised there was another girl, of a similar age to me, in the cot diagonally opposite. She stared at me saying nothing and I stared back.

We were left on our own for hours. There was only the ceiling and walls to look at. I didn't want to be here. I turned to my side and sucked my fingers, retreating to my own little world, where I was back in the ward with the other children. The other girl and I didn't speak to each other.

A nurse arrived with either a meal or a bedpan and was gone again. There was no-one to talk to. I grew lethargic, and often ignored the nurses, and the food. If I didn't eat it, they didn't care, unlike the previous hospital rules.

We stayed in bed all day. No-one came to dress us or for me to get my callipers on. The callipers remained under the bed, gathering dust. There was no schooling, no-one to visit, or entertain us, or just to speak to us.

My father arrived and I was so pleased to see him. I thought I'd been forgotten. He talked about me coming home and I now said 'Yes, I want to come home', even though it didn't mean anything to me. I didn't like it in there. Sometimes the other girl shouted at me to look at her, but we had nothing to say to each other. I don't know why we didn't speak. There was something forbidding about the whole place. It made you want to whisper.

My father turned up with Kath. She brought me two lovely books, with pictures that popped up as you turned the pages. I thought they were lovely and the lady asked me to take good care of them.

A man came in, handcuffed, with policemen on either side. This caused quite a commotion. He didn't stay long. He left a lovely doll with the other little girl. I was quite jealous, as I'd often asked my father for a doll, but still didn't have one.

When they'd all gone, the girl asked if she could look at my books, in exchange for a look at her doll. I looked in horror as the girl began to tear my books up into tiny pieces. I shouted for her to stop, but she continued to tear them up. The nurse returned and the girl demanded her doll back. With the doll returned, I now had nothing. I knew I would be in trouble.

I was in that room for four months and in that time neither of us ever left that room. We didn't get dressed, nor get out of bed. We were mostly just left to ourselves. It would've helped if we could at least have been friends. Every hour was the same and the hours dragged by with no stimulation. We were each locked into our own misery. Looking back, I wondered how long the other girl had been there. Maybe she had forgotten how to chat. I only chatted when my father came and she didn't even have that.

In November, I spent my seventh birthday in that room. A photo of me appeared in the local Taunton newspaper with an article about having to spend my second birthday away from home. The birthday cards came flooding in – I had over two hundred.

Auntie Gladys came to visit and gave me a birthday present from my father and Kath. They were getting ready for their marriage. It was the doll I'd been waiting for! She was made of pink fur with a plastic face sewn-in, plastic hands and shiny blue plastic shoes. I had always wanted a doll I could hug, as most of them were made of hard plastic. This doll was soft and I really could hug her. I adored her and named her Mary. The new lady, Kath, had chosen her.

On 1st December, 1956, my father remarried and he and Kath went to Scotland for their honeymoon. I knew nothing about this.

Just before Christmas, my father turned up. They had come to take me home. Someone found a dress for me. The knickers were lost. My father grabbed my callipers from under the bed, all covered in dust. He gathered me up and carried me out of the room into the waiting ambulance.

I didn't even say 'Goodbye' to the other girl. I've often wondered what happened to her. I'm not sure if I knew her name. She'd been there quite a while on her own before I came, and now she was on her own again. My family had rescued me, but who was going to rescue her?

I was going home – wherever this was. On the way home, I asked why the new lady was with us. My father said that they were now married and she would be my new mother. That didn't mean anything to me either.

CHAPTER 11

GOING HOME

Any concept of family life had long faded away. It had been replaced by hospital life. I had all I needed, I didn't need a mother or father anymore, they weren't part of my life. Any love and affection had been replaced by a strict regime which I was now used to.

My new mother was a complete stranger to me apart from the odd visit. My father was also a stranger to me in many ways; I'd seen him for two hours every week. It had taken my father all day to get to the hospital to visit me, but for me two hours was hardly anything in the busy schedule of hospital life.

I looked out of the ambulance window as it carried me home, and saw such a vast expanse of countryside. The hospital had been the centre of my universe. I'd forgotten another world existed outside. Although the hospital environment was harsh, I'd felt safe there. I was nervous of where I was going next. My father often spoke of home but it meant nothing to me. The children's ward was my home.

The ambulance came to a stop and everyone sighed with relief, except me. To everyone else it was home. My father announced *'We're home!'* I looked out of the window and saw a house but recognised nothing. My father lifted me out and carried me towards the front door.

It all looked so small inside. Everything felt strange; there was nothing I knew or recognised. Stuart appeared and said 'Hello,' and then quickly vanished. Stuart and I were still virtually strangers. We'd only met a few times over nearly two years.

This was the moment my father had been waiting for – to bring his daughter home. He smiled at me, and at his new wife. My new mother had enabled him to bring me home, but I knew nothing about this. I stayed silent. I felt alone and confused.

My father carried me into the first room on the left, where he put me on a bed. They'd brought the bed downstairs and put it in the front room. The room looked so small and dark. It reminded me of the dimly-lit room I'd just come from, and had already spent so much time in. Perhaps if I'd been kept more aware of the outside world, it wouldn't have been such a shock. If families had been made more welcome at the children's ward, I would've thought more about being part of a family, but that'd been taken from me. I don't think my father and new mother understood at all how I felt.

Once again, my whole world had been turned upside down.

Neither of them knew me or who I was now. Hospital life had changed me. At a young age I had to become tough and fight my corner. I'd learnt to lash out and if necessary scream to get attention. Consequently, I was wary of all adults; I saw them as unpredictable. Adults inflicted hardship. Nothing made me cry anymore, it had been a hard lesson to learn for a young child, but now I was in control. Now I wouldn't give anyone the satisfaction of thinking they'd hurt me. Instead of crying, I'd learnt to be, basically, a horrible child if cornered. It was the only way I'd survived on my own.

If anyone had tried to give me any affection, I wouldn't have recognised it. I would pull back, seeing any closeness as a threat. My new parents didn't see this.

I had no clothes. My new mother put me in one of her nightdresses for the night.

They turned out the light. I was completely alone, there wasn't even the girl in the opposite corner. I missed her already, even though we never really spoke. I wasn't sure if I liked home, it wasn't how I thought it would be.

CHAPTER 12

My New Mother

I woke up in my new bed. I was on my own. I could hear music coming from another room, then the door opened and my new mother walked in briskly. 'I've come to get you up,' she said as she approached me. I panicked at her tone of voice. I didn't want her to touch me, and replied quickly 'I want a nurse, I'm not letting you touch me.'

My new mother stood in the middle of the room and said, 'There are no nurses, only me, so you have no choice.' I responded the only way I knew: I noticed that one of my boots was within my reach. I picked it up and threw it at her with as much strength as I could muster.

I was surprised at how far the boot travelled. It missed her face with less than an inch to spare. We both glared at each other. Then, as quickly as she'd appeared, she was gone, slamming the door behind her. The volume of the music increased in the other room.

I waited in bed, wondering what would happen next. My father had gone to work as usual and Stuart had gone to school. I'd been cornered, and behaved as though I was still in the ward. I'd become an unruly child, it was how I had learnt to survive. I needed taming, but I also needed love.

After a while, the door opened and my new mother marched into the room. 'Are you ready to get up now?' was all she said, and I nodded. She picked up my callipers and looked at them. She had no idea how they fitted. She'd never watched anyone dress me, and I'd not worn callipers for nearly four months. They felt strange.

The nurses had dressed me quickly and ignored any protest I made that the callipers were pinching me. I looked at my new mother as she fiddled with the straps. It was as strange for her as it was for me. I only had the dress I came home with and that only just fitted me.

At last, I was dressed.

My new mother lifted me off the bed, stood me up, and let go, expecting me to stand. I immediately collapsed and fell on the floor. I was as surprised as she was. She looked at me, annoyed. She picked me up from the floor and told me to stand still. As soon as she let go, of course, I fell down again, just as before.

I'd forgotten how to stand and how to walk. In the four months I'd lain in the room, with no walking practise, I'd become much weaker. In the ward the physiotherapist had come every day to help me to practise walking. This had all gone to waste. I'd not realised this was going to happen.

My new mother thought I was playing up. Grabbing me under the arms, she lifted me through to the lounge and dumped me onto the settee, and marched away to the kitchen. I knew that she was cross. I was confused, I really thought that I could walk.

I couldn't move, my callipers didn't bend at the knee and just stuck out in front of me. I couldn't get on or off the settee. I looked around me at the living room which was now used all the time. There was a settee and armchair, and a couple of pieces of furniture. From the settee, the window faced the alleyway brick wall.

There was nothing to do, no one to speak to, and no toys to play with. I got bored. I leaned back and sucked my two fingers, my habit as my only source of comfort. I also bit my nails, as no-one had ever cut them.

Suddenly, my fingers were ripped from my mouth. I hadn't seen her coming. 'You'll soon learn not to do that,' she said. 'You can stop biting your nails as well.' She disappeared to the kitchen again. I was so used to sucking my fingers I didn't realise what I was doing, and before long she did the same thing again. 'I'll put salt on your fingers if you do it again.' I asked for Mary, my doll. I hugged her and nibbled her fingers instead.

I wanted the toilet. There was a step from the living room down to the dining room, then another step into the kitchen and through the bathroom in order to get to the outside toilet. The walls of the toilet were whitewashed, with a green door, which led out to the garden. My new mother had to lift me under the arms and carry me to the outside toilet. I had never tried sitting on the toilet with my callipers on before. My legs were straight and immediately fell to the floor, trying to drag me with them. It was all I could do not to fall off, and the callipers pinched my skin as I sat there. I was so ill-prepared for life outside of hospital.

I remained sitting on the settee, with nothing to do, for hours. I was so bored. In the afternoon I noticed some ribbon and a pair of scissors. The ribbon was probably for my hair. I had used scissors previously, forgetting how they had got me into trouble before, with the hot water bottle episode. I proceeded to cut the ribbon up into tiny pieces.

I was happily cutting up the ribbon when suddenly I was flying through the air. Without warning, my mother had lifted me off the settee, slapped my bottom hard and I landed with a thud, back onto the settee. My heart was pounding as I tried to make sense of it all. I looked up and saw my new mother glowering at me. I stared at her to stop myself from crying but my eyelids did prick with tears.

I had to be brave.

She had seen me cut up the ribbon, become angry and responded very quickly. There'd been no words and no warning. It'd all happened so quickly, it didn't seem real, except that my bottom hurt. We glared at each other, not saying anything. I'd learnt from the ward that if I glared at someone, not only did it stop me from crying, but the other person usually backed off. Suddenly, my new mother grabbed the scissors and marched back to the kitchen. She was so angry with me.

I'd never been hit before. I'd been punished a lot but never hit, and it hurt! My new mother scared me. I was proud of myself that I hadn't cried. In hospital, crying was always forbidden. Maybe if I had cried she would've come over and comforted me and we might've forged some kind of link. This was my mother's first experience of looking after children. She was struggling with the new situation and tackled the problem as she saw fit. I wasn't used to parents being in control.

Even though I had no words for it, I needed to be loved. I needed someone to put their arms around me and tell me that they cared and that it was alright. My new mother thought I needed to be taught a lesson. She saw me as a child who'd been spoilt in hospital and needed discipline. No-one outside the hospital had any idea how tough life had been in hospital. I was unruly, but I was behaving in the way I had learnt to survive.

Now I was learning a new type of punishment. I decided that I needed to keep a look-out. I had to know when my mother was coming from the kitchen into the living room. I didn't want to be caught out again without warning. She walked so fast, it made me jump when she approached. That day, I continued to sit on the settee and hug Mary, whilst keeping one eye on the door.

When my father came home from work, my new mother said to him, 'I thought you said that she could walk?'

'Yes, she can,' my father replied.

Of course, neither of them had appreciated that after months of being in bed, I'd forgotten how to walk. I heard her tell my father how hard it'd been for her to cope with me. Then she mentioned me cutting-up the ribbon and how I must learn to behave. My father kept quiet.

I'd sat on the settee all day with nothing to do and no-one to talk to. I'd been shouted at and, for the first time that I could remember, I'd been hit. It hadn't been a very good start. If my real mother had survived, maybe she would've noticed the changes in me. She might've picked me up and hugged me, letting me kick out and hit out until I finally realised I could surrender and accept her love. Hopefully, she might've noticed how I was behaving in hospital and investigated. My father was struggling to cope and had no idea.

My new mother didn't know me. She didn't know that underneath I wanted to be a nice child. She was unsure of me and had never been a parent before. As I glared at her, my new mother backed away. She'd received a difficult upbringing and had used this as a basis to bring us up. If I was going to be difficult, *she* could be more difficult. We'd created a barrier between us. This mother had sent me postcards with lots of hugs and kisses on. Maybe she wanted to hug me, but I was wary. She may want to hit me instead; I wasn't going to give her the option. This didn't bode well at all.

CHAPTER 13

Adjusting to Life at Home

The next day I stayed silent while my mother lifted my legs into the callipers and tightened the straps. She didn't try to stand me up, but lifted me under the arms and carried me to the settee in the lounge. My hair was long and tangled. My mother couldn't get me to a hairdressers, so she reached for a pair of scissors and cut my hair herself. She wasn't used to cutting hair but anything was better than the tangled mess in front of her. I wasn't used to looking into a mirror, and accepted how I looked.

My hair needed washing but my mother had a problem: the bathroom basin was upstairs, there was only the high kitchen sink. I couldn't stand at the sink long enough without collapsing. When sitting down I was too low. I lacked the balance to lean back over a bowl of water without sliding down. My mother had an idea. The outside garden path sloped downwards so she laid me on the path just outside the kitchen with my head pointing down the slope. She knelt beside me with a bowl of warm water, lathered my hair and rinsed it letting the water run down the path. It solved the problem for the moment, although it always had to be a sunny day, with time for my hair to dry.

Another first for a very long time was a bath. I hadn't seen a bath in hospital and was only used to blanket baths. The bathroom had been added to the kitchen and it was cold in there in the winter. My father brought in an old tin bath and put it by the fire in the living room in the evening. They fetched buckets of hot water from the kitchen to fill the tin bath and then my father lifted me in. I loved being in hot water. It was the only time my feet and legs felt warm. My circulation was poor due to my paralysis. There was no central heating and I soon acquired chilblains on my feet and legs. They were so painful and itched as my feet warmed up by the fire. No amount of blankets helped.

I had no clothes apart from the dress I came home in, and that barely fitted me. Money was short. Stuart badly needed new clothes as well. My mother went to the first jumble sale she could find and arrived home with a pile of clothes to alter. Every evening after finishing the chores, she sat at the sewing machine adjusting the clothes to fit us.

I'd come out of hospital a few days before Christmas, so there was a big rush to get everything ready. My mother bought strips of gummed paper and taught me how to make paper chains to decorate the rooms. I watched in wonder as my mother explained that on Christmas Eve evening she had to leave a mince pie outside for Father Christmas and a bowl of milk for the reindeer.

Christmas Day arrived. I found a stocking at the end of my bed from Father Christmas, full of presents. We all gathered together to open our presents, and my father and new mother smiled at each other. They'd achieved what was once thought impossible, they'd brought us together again as a family. My parents gave me a small carry cot which my

TO PADDLE MY FEET

mother had made. It was fashioned from two shoe boxes stuck together with blue Fablon, and complete with handles. My mother had made a bed with sheets and blankets and a small doll to fit. I loved it. It was just the right size for me to manage and it was light enough so that I could carry it around with me. I spent hours making and re-making the bed, and putting the doll to bed. I played with it so much that in time the carry cot finally disintegrated.

I was given more toys, but I still played with my favourites, especially Mary, the cloth doll I received when I was 7 during the time I was in hospital. My mother patched her, and re-patched her, to stop her wearing out. When she had any spare time she would knit clothes for my toys; something that I probably didn't appreciate at the time, but I do now.

Every Christmas, I was given a sugar mouse with my presents. This was something my father always looked out for and still bought for me as an adult at Christmas time. I was not fond of the sugary taste but I always looked forward to getting one. I don't know if there was any significance, I never asked. It obviously made him happy to give me something quirky like this.

I had to learn to walk again. My parents struggled to keep lifting me around. Every time I needed the toilet someone had to lift me down the steps to the outside toilet and back again. Sometime I found it painful as they tried to find a grip and cope with the heavy callipers. They said they needed a wheelchair to take me out. There were no free wheelchairs on the National Health in those days and the hospital wanted £50. That was a lot of money then. My parents didn't have the money (my father earned just £517 per annum in

1957, around £10.00 a week, as foreman – I have the letter confirming his new pay from British Rail) so they continued to lift me around while they tried to save for the wheelchair. My father did carpentry work for other people in the evenings to bring in extra cash.

With my ongoing therapy, an ambulance took me to the Outpatient Physiotherapy Department in Musgrove Park Hospital. I was stood between two parallel bars. I held onto the bars while they taught me how to swing my legs. They rolled a football towards me and encouraged me to swing my foot and hit it. I had exercises to improve my arms and balance. I had lost a lot of strength lying in bed for four months. The rest of the time I just sat on the settee in the living room. Lifting me was kept to a minimum. I was bored. I missed the hospital ward and the children. I hated sitting on my own with no-one to talk to. My father and Stuart were always out and my mother constantly busy.

Sometimes I could catch a glimpse and hear the children playing outside in the gardens and communal path which connected all the gardens. They often rode their bicycles along the path. The older children went to the recreation ground further down the street. My mother tried to encourage some of the children in to play with me, but as I couldn't move they soon got bored and would disappear.

We had an elderly neighbour next door who hated most people, especially children. She threw buckets of water onto the mud-pack path to stop the children playing. One day our father watched her walk down the path with a bucket of water. He quickly picked up a bucket of water and walked down to the path to meet her. He said 'If you throw that bucket of water on the path, I'm going to throw this bucket of water over you.' She stared at my father and dashed to her back door. She often rested with a window blind almost down, but just enough for her to spy out of the window looking for trouble. There were very few cars around then, but when someone dared to park a car outside her house, she'd cover the car in whitewash, the stuff used to paint outside toilets.

Stuart was either train-spotting or playing with friends. We had a long, narrow garden which backed onto the railway track. Stuart loved looking through the bars, adding train numbers to his train-spotting book. As he grew older, he walked to the train station to continue his interest. He had a huge model train set, taking up most of his bedroom. Stuart and I had grown apart and we still didn't know what to say to each other.

Creating a home was more difficult than my mother thought. She rushed around trying to provide everything we needed, eager to prove that she could cope with her new life. In the new year she became ill with pleurisy. The doctor said she needed to slow down and take care of herself. He said in Somerset people work at a slower pace, not the fast pace Londoners were used to. For her, there just seemed so much to do.

I spent so much time alone. They had wanted me home, but now I was home it seemed that, mission completed, they could get on with family life as they saw it. I day-dreamed about being back in the Children's Ward and playing with the other children. I wanted to go back there.

I was wary of my mother. I backed away if she came near. She had hit me once, and she might hit me again. A quick succession of reprimands had taught me not to suck my fingers or bite my nails. Where were the hugs and kisses she had put on the postcards she sent me in hospital? I think she found my behaviour challenging, I wasn't the loveable child she thought I would be. She didn't seem to know that I needed to be hugged and comforted. Neither of us knew what to do.

CHAPTER 14

Education Begins

I was seven years old and l had forgotten how to read or write. I was rarely in the Children's Ward during the few hours of hospital school lessons; I didn't even know the letters of the alphabet. I had forgotten everything. No-one had queried my lack of education. There was so much else going on in my life – getting me up and being mobile had to come first.

The education authorities wanted to send me away to a special school for disabled children; the local schools weren't accessible to any disabled child, and any schools approached were adamant they couldn't take me. My parents were determined to keep me at home, they were against a special school.

The Local Authority agreed to provide one hour's tuition each day. A retired teacher came to our home, but the hour soon passed. During this time, my mother raced off to the local school to claim the free bottle of milk the other children had at the time. With so little tuition, progress was slow, and I wasn't used to learning. My mother decided to take control. 'You are going to learn,' she said. After the session, my mother carried me out to the kitchen and sat me on a kitchen chair. I found it hard to sit on an ordinary chair, my legs were heavy and my callipers just fell to the floor taking me with them. My mother placed my legs on another chair so that I didn't move. She put a tray on my lap with some paper and drew some letters. I spent hours copying the different letters of the alphabet and learning how to pronounce them while my mother carried on with her chores. She taught me simple arithmetic and I had to repeat the times-tables every day. To begin with, nothing made sense, but gradually I improved.

My mother researched school history programmes on the radio and I had to sit and listen. She then asked me questions about the programme. My mother was determined that I was going to catch up with other children my age. I wasn't so keen. Every day I did the same lessons. There was no fun attached, and my mother had little patience if I got answers wrong. I wasn't used to seeing many books. There were very few books in the hospital or at home. My father was never interested in books, he said they were a waste of time. By fourteen he had left school and was training to be a carpenter. He was proud of the fact that he'd never read a book in his life. We had the Daily Mail every day and he bought the local Somerset County Gazette which he always read.

If my father was working locally he always came home for his midday meal. This meant that my mother was often cooking while teaching me. Stuart stayed at school for his main meal. After our meal, my mother lifted me into the living room and turned on the television. I was allowed to see Watch with Mother. I looked forward to this every day as we had no television in hospital. We saw Picture Book on Monday, Andy Pandy on Tuesday, Bill and Ben the

Flowerpot Men on Wednesday, Rag, Tag and Bobtail on Thursday, and my favourite, The Wooden Tops on Friday. These programmes were intended for younger children, but I really enjoyed them. Then the test card came onto the screen with an ongoing noise. In those days there was no afternoon television. My sessions resumed as my mother returned to her afternoon chores. Progress was slow, but I was improving. I didn't enjoy the sessions, they were relentless. My brother came home from school, put his school books down, and went out to play. I wanted to go out and play as well, but I couldn't escape.

CHAPTER 15

HELLO WHEELCHAIR!

My wheelchair arrived. It was a basic design and didn't fold-up. It wouldn't fit through any of the doorways into the front room or lounge, so the wheelchair had to be kept in the narrow hallway. This meant I could only use it for outside. Everyone had to squeeze by its bulk to get in or out of the front door.

Twice a week, my mother wrapped me up well, and pushed me into town for the shopping. The quickest way was down a very steep hill, locally named Cake Hill. The nickname was because there used to be a cake factory nearby.

Most of the local shops had steps. I was left outside, along with all the children in prams and pushchairs, while my mother went into the small shops. There were never any worries as there is today about leaving children outside. There were no supermarkets then. I remember sitting outside the butcher shop and there was always sawdust on the floor of the shop.

On one occasion, I was outside a shop in my wheelchair and my mother was approaching the entrance. Someone passed by and asked my mother if I was spastic. This was a very old term for anyone with Cerebral Palsy. I heard her and thought that she must've asked if I was plastic. There used to be plastic models of disabled children outside shops with slots for donation money. I thought she meant I was one of those. I shouted back to her 'I'm not plastic!' The lady hurried away, and I heard my mother chuckle as she entered the shop.

It took my mother all her strength to push me back uphill, with all the shopping too. If there was any money left over, my mother bought a lardy cake, a favourite for my father.

On sunny days, my parents wanted me to be in the back garden and meet other children. In order to achieve this, my father had to push the wheelchair out of the front door and along to the end of the terrace houses. Then he pushed the wheelchair to the back gardens and onto the communal mud-packed path and back to our garden, ready for me to sit in. My father had to repeat the procedure to store my wheelchair.

The wheelchair also had a negative side. From my experience, anyone sitting in a wheelchair is less likely to be hugged than if you are a child standing. People aren't so likely to bend down to wheelchair-height to give you a kiss. Sometimes people tapped me on the head as though I was a pet dog. That really annoyed me, or they would bend down and speak to me really slowly as though I was an idiot. It was rude for a child to say anything, so I had to keep quiet. When anyone goes out with a child, you make them hold hands for safety, but also for re-assurance. That doesn't happen when you're in a wheelchair. It's like a missing link, a lack of connection. Maybe if I held my mother's hand we might have forged a link of some kind. Anything would've helped, but it didn't happen.

You might think we forged a link whenever I was lifted. I was heavy to lift and my parents often moaned about having to cope with this. Being lifted was often ungainly and painful. Now I was walking more, I only had to be lifted down the steps. We were together but I didn't feel any connection. My parents were trying their hardest to make me part of the family, but I didn't feel loved. No-one had put a comforting arm around me. I knew my parents came from an era where people didn't express their feelings. I found it so hard to be part of a family.

My mother was told that I could easily gain weight through lack of mobility, so to be careful about what I ate. Every morning I was given a bowl of All Bran for breakfast. I hated it, and complained to begin with. My mother said that if I didn't eat it she would give me more. There was never a choice.

Meals were nourishing but my mother rarely included pastry for pies or anything fattening. Sometimes she made a cake for a treat. Food sold in the shops was still limited and fairly basic. Food rationing hadn't long been lifted, and most families had gardens or allotments and relied on the produce for their meals. We usually had the same meals each week: Roast on a Sunday, with the left-over cold meat for another meal. Fridays was always fish day. There was no fridge or freezer, everything was kept in the cool pantry.

My father was outside gardening one day when he cut his thumb badly, which needed stitches. My mother ran over to ask a neighbour if they could drive him to the hospital, telling my father to change into more decent clothes. My father hated the sight of blood and passed out. My mother was determined that he would go to hospital looking respectable and carried on trying to change him while he was out cold. He came round enough to be bundled into the car. I was told to stay in the kitchen, but I saw it all.

We often had baked beans for a snack or for tea. One day I was in the kitchen and saw a saucepan with baked beans warming up. I couldn't resist the temptation to dip my finger into the sauce and lick my finger. I turned around and saw my mother watching me. She asked me if I had touched the baked beans. I was scared by the way she looked at me, and shook my head. I knew I had lied but I was frightened by the look on her face. She marched up to me and slapped me hard across the face, turned away and stormed off. I felt guilty, as I knew I'd lied. I wanted to say 'sorry' but she'd gone.

Before I caught polio, my mother was close to her sisters and their families, and we often met up for picnics. Her sisters, Gladys, Hilda and Olive and their mother, my grandmother, kept in touch while I was in hospital. Now I had a new mother, my parents were keen for me to accept her as my mother. They thought that in time I would forget that I had another family and all would be well.

Although my relatives wanted to continue seeing me and Stuart, my mother saw this as a threat. We did occasionally meet up. My cousin Anne remembers her father driving over to pick us all up, to take us back to their country house in North Curry. Anne took me for a stroll in my wheelchair along Oxen Lane. It was the season for primroses; she can remember pushing me close to the hedge so that I could pick some. Gradually the visits stopped. My mother said there was never a convenient time.

But Aunt Gladys was determined to keep in touch. She sent me birthday cards and little notes and had visited me in hospital. When I was much older, I visited Aunt Gladys, and she talked to me about my mother.

Although I can't remember my birth mother, somehow I've always known I had another mother who loved me. I can't explain, I just knew. I was never allowed to speak about my mother, and there were no photos, but she was there in my heart.

Many years later, a spiritual lady said that a little old dumpy lady was looking after me. My grandmother, who was small and dumpy, died soon after my mother; I think she couldn't cope with the tragedy. I believed her as I had always felt this myself. Don't ask me how I knew. I think if my parents had realised that I needed to know about my real mother, I would've been more likely to accept my new mother.

CHAPTER 16

HOSPITAL AGAIN

Six months later, I visited my consultant. He was concerned about my spine which was showing signs of a curvature. I don't think months of sitting on a settee with my legs stretched straight out had helped. He wanted to make a back support for me. He said 'I think we'd better have her in hospital again.'

I hadn't expected him to say that. My face lit up and I beamed at him. I was going back to the children's ward where I wanted to be. I was so excited and eagerly helped my mother to pack my case. This time I had some clothes.

When we arrived at the hospital, the porter found me a wheelchair. It was huge, but I didn't care. I raced on ahead and into the ward. I looked for Pauline and there she was, still in the ward. She saw me and called me over. We chatted away. It was as though I'd never left.

My parents had a talk with the Sister in her office, and then came back to say goodbye. They called my name from the doorway of the ward. I turned around to look at them and then turned away to play. When I looked around again, they were gone.

Sister Mumford came into the ward and smiled at me. I smiled back and felt a surge of warmth and comfort. A porter recognised me. He came up to me and ruffled my hair, whilst saying something to me that made me laugh. I couldn't remember laughing much at home. I was so glad to be back. I was like a tiger who'd been let out of its cage. I tore around the ward in the wheelchair. I was free and I had children to talk to and play with. I'd missed the company of children, and there was room to move around with a wheelchair, so I very happily took advantage of it.

I went to the splint room to have measurements taken for my back support. The support was similar to the type of corset the Victorian ladies wore. There were long laces which took forever to do-up and they had to be pulled tight to create a support for my spine.

It made it even more difficult for me to try and sit up with my legs straight out in front of me. Every day I went to the Physiotherapist Department to practise my walking. There was a strap each side of the brace, which they attached to the top of my calliper. It meant that I didn't lean over so much to move my legs. I hated wearing my new spinal support, but I had to get used to it. They showed me how I could climb up a step by swinging my leg forward. I found it really hard to stand on one leg and try to put the other leg on the step, and then heave myself up. However, I was beginning to manage shallow steps.

I spent more time at the hospital school now, but as with so many children in the ward, I still hadn't learnt enough to properly understand some of the lessons. I got up to all kinds of mischief around the ward. Whenever my parents came to visit, they were asked to go and report to the Sister's office. I was a different child to the one they knew at home. I'd spent the last six months mainly sitting on a settee, and needed to play. The other children weren't going to run away from me, we were all in the same situation. I found that there was no solitary confinement anymore, it'd been stopped.

While there, I never missed my parents. I'd found it so difficult to re-connect with family life. Maybe it was too late after spending so long in hospital. I had to sit by my bed while my parents came to visit me. This was usually at the weekend, as my father didn't get time off from work anymore. As soon as they left, I played with the other children. I stayed in hospital for about eight weeks, and then I had to go home wearing my new brace. I was very reluctant to leave my friends.

I was back on the settee again as the family got on with their chores. Now it was even more uncomfortable to sit wearing a brace and callipers. My walking had improved but I still couldn't climb the steep steps into the different rooms. I tried to swing my leg forward but it kept hitting the step. I still couldn't get off the settee by myself, so there I stayed, stuck in the one place I didn't want to be.

After receiving reports from the hospital about my wild behaviour, my mother decided that I needed more discipline.

CHAPTER 17

BIRTHDAY CELEBRATIONS

It was my eighth birthday. My mother had invited some local children around for a small birthday party. I watched in awe as my mother put a tablecloth on the table, laying out plates of jam and banana sandwiches. There were also plates of iced cakes and dishes of jelly. I couldn't wait for the children to arrive and the party to begin. I was all ready in the new dress my mother had made for me.

My mother asked Stuart to tidy up the living room and to make sure it was all ready. I was standing by the table, leaning against one of the armchairs. Stuart, without realising, moved the armchair. I immediately lost my balance and started falling backwards. Instinctively, I reached out to grab something to save myself – it happened to be the tablecloth! Along with the tablecloth came all the food, plates and dishes.

I sat on the floor with everything from the table all over and around me. My mother rushed in to see what'd happened. I thought she was going to shout at me, but all she said was 'Thank goodness I didn't put the teapot on the table!' She quickly retrieved most of the food and made it look as though nothing had happened. She stood me up and brushed me down just in time for the children to arrive. Nothing was said, and I don't think the children ever realised what'd happened. We had a lovely party.

I was getting to know some of the local children, and sometimes they came to play with me. I found it difficult as, naturally, they wanted to run around. I still lost my balance and fell if I moved suddenly. We played ball games, but again I had to be careful that I didn't reach too far to catch it and so lose my balance and fall. It was nice to be with other children but they gradually got bored and didn't stay for long.

Now that I was eight years old, the Education Authorities said I could have two hours' tuition a day instead of only the one hour. I still sat in the kitchen after the tuition and carried on with my schooling. I could read basic words and sentences. We didn't have any children's books for my reading ability, so my mother wrote out sentences for me to read. She taught me how to write a letter with all the punctuation. One day a neighbour came around with a dish of strawberries as a treat. They looked lovely. My mother said I had to write a thank you letter before eating the strawberries. I forget how many letters she tore up saying I'd made a mistake.

I hated those strawberries!

Any pocket money had to be earned. My mother made a list of jobs to do with the amount we would earn written beside them. Most jobs were worth a farthing or a ha'penny. Stuart did the more active jobs, but my mother made sure I did some.

I laid the table and helped to wipe the dishes. I cleaned the silver chromed cutlery and cut the salt blocks up into chunk-size pieces, putting them into a jar ready for use. At fruit picking time I had to top and tail the gooseberries, and generally get any fruit ready to make jam or preserves in bottles. If my mother thought I might eat any, I had to whistle. She said that was what she had to do as a child.

I collected my hard-earned pennies. Every time we went into town, we had to pass a bicycle shop. The shop also sold miniature plastic farmyard animals. I was allowed to go in and buy one of these animals.

Every evening we switched on the television to watch the news. Richard Baker was the newsreader. I thought he could see me as I got undressed and ready for bed in the warm living room. I wanted to hide behind the settee. My parents tried to convince me otherwise.

I watched an interpretation of Aladdin and the Lamp. It showed him entering a cave of water, which was covered with waving hands trying to grab him. I became scared that unseen hands could grab me. I had to check the whole bedroom before going to bed for some months after.

Every week a volunteer pushed me to Brownies at Rowbarton. I had been a Brownie in hospital and really enjoyed it. I remember being carried onto a coach for an outing, a new experience for me.

My mother thought I ought to have some hobbies. She got me interested in saving postage stamps and bought me an album. She helped me look out for unusual ones. Another hobby was to learn how to knit. The problem was that I am left-handed and my mother was right-handed. If I made a mistake, she found it hard to put right. She decided that I needed to learn how to knit right-handed. It was like knitting backwards for me and was very confusing. She suggested that I knitted squares to make a blanket and asked neighbours to bring any spare wool. It passed the time, but I didn't enjoy it. I wanted to be off the settee and running around.

I could now climb the step into each room. My father decided that it was time I slept in my bedroom upstairs, so I had to climb the stairs. My father stood behind me and lifted one of my legs to the next step, helping me to push myself up the step. It was a slow process. I had to come down the stairs backwards. Someone had to make sure that my foot landed on the step below before I lowered myself down. I was scared of falling down the stairs and could never do this on my own.

A gentleman wrote to my parents. He had heard about my brother and me becoming disabled, and asked if he could write to us. He enclosed a fairy story he had typed. My mother sat down and read me the story. It was the first story I had heard for ages and I really enjoyed it. The fairy stories came regularly; they came from the Grimm's Fairy Story book, and were signed 'Uncle Donald'.

Uncle Donald and his wife came to visit, and took Stuart and me shopping. They showered us with gifts and toys. I couldn't stop talking about our shopping trip when I got home. Uncle Donald wrote more letters and they came for another visit. They brought me the most gorgeous doll I could ever imagine. I couldn't take my eyes off her. They wanted Stuart to go to Scotland for a holiday and my parents were considering this. But, one day, a neighbour knocked on the front door. She'd listened to a radio programme warning about a couple trying to entice children away, who then disappeared. My parents realised how little they knew about the couple and confronted them on their return the next day. Although they tried to deny it, they rushed away and we never heard from them again. My parents were so upset that they could've been fooled like that.

As they left, my doll was thrust into their arms.

CHAPTER 18

A Broken Leg

My consultant wanted to see how I walked. During the visit, I was proud to show him how much I'd improved, and walked across the room. I tried too hard and managed to do the splits right in front of him.

Walking was always a struggle, being propped up by metal supports which dug into me, with straps that pinched me, and a spinal support which rubbed me raw. I often over-balanced and fell. Why was it so important that I had to walk? It was the adults who made the decisions. No-one ever said 'Let's have a day without having to wear any supports'. That was simply never allowed.

They were now making callipers that bent at the knee, which the consultant wanted me to try. It meant another visit to the Children's Ward. I began to realise that these visits were going to be regular, which made me happy. I was soon chatting to Pauline again and getting to know the other children.

I had new callipers made with a hinge each side. I had to lean forward to hold my leg up while I undid the hinges with the other hand to bend the knee. It was difficult to lean forward with my brace, and I struggled to cope. The consultant hoped it would put less pressure on my spine, which he saw had curved more. The Consultant suggested just having a hinge on one side of the calliper to help. He also wanted me to sleep in a plaster bed to keep my back straight at night. In order to construct the plaster bed I had to stand between two metal pillars, with my callipers on. Then a padded strap was placed around my neck and under my chin, with a rope attached. The rope was on a pulley system and the rope was then pulled as hard as possible. They wanted my spine to be as straight as they could get it. It felt like the nearest thing to hanging. My feet just touched the floor, and the neck support dug into my face.

They wrapped wet Plaster of Paris all around me from the hips to as far up as they could go. I had to remain in that position until the plaster dried, which was about half an hour. Once the plaster was dry they had to saw-off the cast. I just hoped the saw didn't touch me, but they said it was a special saw. Finally, the pulley was released.

They used the plaster mould for me to lie in. The plaster mould was padded and straps were attached so that I could be strapped into the cast at night. I hated wearing this as it meant I could never move, and I always had to sleep on my back. This process had to be repeated every six months while I was growing, which meant continuous visits to the hospital.

The corset brace was replaced with a leather brace. I was stretched again for the mould to be made. They filled it in and used it to shape the leather brace, which was stronger. The corset I had worn had some kind of flexibility, this brace had none.

Making things worse, my feet were beginning to curve in. I had splints made for my feet to keep them straight at night. It was like an ankle boot with metal rods either side attached to a leather strap at the knee. There was a protruding metal spike above my toes which were open. A spring was attached from the end of the spike up to the knee; this forced my feet into a straight and upright position. I had to wear callipers and brace during the day, and now I had to wear similar things at night. There was no respite.

No-one ever asked what I thought of everything I had to cope with. My feeling was that this was all done so that I could be accepted into society.

I returned home, together with my new callipers, with one hinge at each knee, my new plaster bed and splints for my feet at night. While I was in hospital, I had received more exercises to help me cope with wearing my new callipers and brace.

One afternoon, I was walking down the garden path, when for some unknown reason I slipped and fell. My right leg hit the dustbin and undid the only hinge of my right calliper, so I fell on a bent leg. I tried to move, but my leg really hurt. My mother picked me up, carried me indoors onto the settee, and called the doctor. I had broken my leg. The doctor said that the calliper was as efficient as any Plaster of Paris; so, after checking that my leg was in the right position, he went away saying that my calliper mustn't come off for at least six weeks. Now I had to sleep on the settee. It had become my new bed. Trust me to fall and undo the only hinge!

Once my leg healed and I could walk again, the consultant said that I needed to return to hospital to have callipers made with a hinge on both sides. This made it more difficult for me to sit down, but made it safer for walking.

Each time I went into hospital, my education suffered as I couldn't keep up with the lessons. I could now just about read, but only books meant for a much younger age group, and I still had no interest in reading. I found it hard to learn in a home environment, with no real stimulus from other children.

I was nine. For a special treat my parents took me to the cinema to see Walt Disney's film Lady and the Tramp. I had never been to the cinema before to see a film in colour. Wheelchairs weren't allowed; in those days they were a fire hazard. I couldn't cope with the downward slope to the seats without falling over. My father picked me up and carried me down the aisle to one of the seats. I usually sat down with my legs out in front of me and would then bend them. I couldn't do this because of the seat in front. My father had to hold me up while my mother undid the hinges and then slide me into the seat.

I loved the story of Lady and the Tramp, but I was so uncomfortable. I had no strength in my legs and the seat wanted to fold up on me all the time. My parents had to lean on each side of the seat. Then the procedure had to be reversed to get me out of the seat. It was a real struggle and I said that I didn't want to go again. It was many years before I went to the cinema once more, when wheelchairs were eventually allowed.

I still had regular physiotherapy exercise at the hospital. The therapist always made the sessions fun, using beanbags and balls. My usual physiotherapist retired during the summer and so I had a new therapist. This new therapist had a different approach; the manipulations were so painful I now hated going. My parents queried the new treatment with the consultant and he just said that I didn't need to go anymore. This wasn't what we expected. I was just so relieved. I never went for physiotherapy ever again.

CHAPTER 19

LONDON

My new mother's family lived in and around the south of London and we occasionally travelled to stay with them. We boarded the steam train to Paddington Station. The underground tubes were not accessible for me, so we took a taxi to Charing Cross. My mother was used to London life and was keen to point out famous landmarks along the way.

Once at Charing Cross, we had to rush to catch our train along with loads of other people. Everyone was running, you had to know where you were going, otherwise there was a risk the train went without you. There was no time to try and get me out of my wheelchair and onto the train. Even when the whistle was blown, people were still trying to board the train and squeeze in.

The only option for me was the guard's van. My father and the guard would heave me into the van as there was no ramp. Then my father had to make a quick dash to get on the same train. My mother and Stuart had already boarded the train.

The guard's van was constantly busy. Sacks of post arrived, as well as crates of chickens, bicycles and anything else which wouldn't fit into a compartment. As the train stopped at different stations along the way, some of the luggage would disappear, and more got thrown in.

I was fascinated watching the guard doing his job, whether blowing a whistle and waving a flag, watching instruments by his seat, making notes or shouting out because people were still trying to board the train as it moved off. As soon as the train stopped at a station, numerous people would come up to the guard asking if this was the right train. Mostly there was a grunt which seemed sufficient for them as they dashed off again.

To begin with, it was a little overpowering, but as I got older I would enjoy talking to the guard. We would very often joke with one another, according to what the guard was like. Sometimes a guard didn't speak, but most were fairly chatty. I quite enjoyed my little bit of independence.

There was no access to the guard's van from the rest of the train, so my parents couldn't come to see if I was alright. They didn't dare get off the train in case it started going without them. Once off the train at Eltham, we walked to a terraced house in Grange Hill. My mother's parents were lovely, known as Nana and Pop, and the house had a warm feel. There was a front room which no-one used much. There was a living room where everything happened, with a small kitchen at the back which led to a back yard and garden.

I slept in a cosy room upstairs. My father had to help me up the stairs. I could curl into a ball to sleep as there was no way we could bring the plaster bed or splints. It felt wonderful.

My new Uncle Ken and Aunt Mariette came around with their children. Uncle Ken was Kath's brother. Their daughter Annette was the eldest, about 12 years old, a few years older than me; then Christine, Claire and Robert. Christine came over to play with me and sometimes Claire came as well. It was so much fun. We made up conjuring tricks and put on performances for the rest of the family.

One day we were leaving home to catch the train to London for the weekend; I was told to sit still on the settee and wait until everyone was ready. It was winter and my mother had put a thick pair of socks over my callipers, which almost reached to the top of my legs, to try and keep my feet warm. Sitting on the settee with nothing to do, I soon got bored, and decided to try and move.

I attempted to get off the settee, but I forgot that the socks made my feet slippery and I landed in a heap on the floor. One leg went under the sideboard and stuck. The other leg caught behind the door, which was almost shut. Pain shot through me and I screamed my head off. My father rushed down the stairs, but found that he couldn't come into the lounge because of the way I was positioned with the fall.

I couldn't move and no-one could come in to help me. My father had to go out of the front door and around the block of terrace houses to the back entrance of our house. The back door was already locked, ready for going away, so he had to prise the lounge window open to climb in and lift me away from the door.

My mother was really cross that I'd moved. She made it clear, none of this had needed to happen; if only I would do as I was told. I wasn't allowed to forget how badly behaved I'd been while we rushed off to catch the train.

During our visits to London we could travel into the city by train for the day to look around. One day we went to the Tower of London. Stuart wanted to see the Crown

Jewels, which were underground, down some very steep and winding steps. My parents said there was no way they could get me down to see the jewels. I had to stay at the top and wait for them. It looked like quite a wait as my parents and brother joined the long, slow queue.

After a while, two Beefeaters came along and chatted to me. They asked me if I'd seen the Crown Jewels. I said no, as my parents had said it wasn't possible. They looked at each other and said, 'We'll soon change that.' They lifted me up, supporting me between them, and off we went towards the steps. With instructions from the Beefeaters of '*Make way, Make way!*' the crowd had no option other than to press themselves against the walls as we descended the steps towards the Crown Jewels. I must've passed my parents and brother, but I was having too good a time to notice.

They then stood me up, and let me lean on them while I gazed at all the jewels. To a small girl it was like entering another world, of magic, full of crowns and glittering swords. I was fascinated, and suddenly noticed my parents coming towards me. One Beefeater said, 'Hurry along there, please.' I wanted to giggle as I decided to ignore them.

I was where they'd said I couldn't go – and I'd got there before them! Not only that, but the Beefeaters told me I could stay as long as I liked. I knew I couldn't stand for too long, so they carried me back up the stairs to daylight and I was back in my chair before my parents arrived. I was so proud of what I'd achieved without any help from my parents.

We were returning home on one occasion at Paddington Station for the train back to Taunton. It was a long journey, so my father lifted me out of the wheelchair and quickly stepped onto the train, putting me on a seat in one of the empty carriages. They left me, to put my wheelchair in the guard's van. A long time passed and I worried that I might be on my own when the train moved. The whistle blew and the train slowly moved out of the station. I was still on my own and stuck on the seat. I was scared at what might be going to happen to me. After a short while, my parents and Stuart arrived. It was a long train and they'd had to walk the entire length of it. My mother told me off for being scared. I hadn't known they were on the train and really thought that I was going to be left on my own. It made me think of being left behind in the old Roman Baths while I was in hospital and how frightened I'd been then.

During the summer holidays, Uncle Ken brought his family to stay. We had to share bedrooms, which was fun, and we would play for hours in the back garden. One day we all went to a Circus in town. It was raining and not everyone had raincoats. We walked through the town in an assortment of attire to keep off the rain. My mother was convinced that passers-by thought we were vagrants, but we didn't care and really enjoyed the Circus.

CHAPTER 20

RAILWAY LIFE

Now that my walking was better and I had a wheelchair, we felt more able to go out as a family. On some weekends, my mother packed a picnic and we walked to Taunton station and boarded a steam train to the coast. We loved going to Dawlish, Teignmouth and Paignton along the south coast. Stuart and I chatted away while we watched the steam train puff its way along the coast. Near the estuary of Star Cross there was always a boat built in the shape of a swan, and each of us tried to be the first person to spot it. Many years later, I saw the same swan boat in a Maritime Museum.

These trips helped us to become a family. It was so nice to be together and have a fun day out. It gave time for Stuart and me to bond as brother and sister. We both loved the steam trains. As trains weren't accessible to me back then, my father would lift me onto the train and then run down the platform to put the wheelchair into the guard's van. On one occasion, we had stopped at a station along the way and I pointed to a wheelchair on the platform which I said looked just like mine. My father looked up and said '*It is* yours!' and as the whistle blew for the train to leave, my father leapt off the train and grabbed the wheelchair. On another journey, we found that the guard's van had been disconnected during the journey. No guard's van, no wheelchair. The wheelchair was returned to us a week later.

Once on the beach we settled down to enjoy ourselves. We were on the beach at Teignmouth one day when it began to rain heavily. My parents quickly wrapped the groundsheet around me and left me sitting on the ground with an umbrella to hold. Then they ran with the wheelchair to stand under the pier. I had great fun sitting there by myself in the rain, waving to my parents and Stuart standing under the pier. Once the rain stopped, they came back and we settled down again.

I was eight in the summer of 1958 and my parents organised our first family holiday. We stayed at the Lantern Hotel in Worthing, which was then owned by the British Polio Fellowship. It was one of the very few hotels adapted for disabled people in those days. Every family staying at the hotel had someone who'd been disabled by polio. It was good to meet and chat with other people who had similar problems. Sometimes we'd felt as though we were the only affected family, trying to cope with a society which wasn't geared for disabled people.

The hotel had a beach hut with a wooden ramp which rolled right down to the sea's edge. I sat at the edge in my swimming costume and splashed around without my brace or callipers. It was a lovely feeling to be free of them. I couldn't swim, but was just happy to stay at the water's edge.

The Hotel owned some old-fashioned wheeled hand-bikes. They had a wheelchair type seat with two wheels at the back and one at the front with hand-pedals to turn. They were too big for me but I insisted on trying them. As I pedalled along the promenade, the hand-bike increased in speed. I was exhilarated by the independence and freedom it gave me.

I felt so free!

I unintentionally gained speed so much that I left my parents and Stuart far behind. For a while I felt fine, but then thought *What if the promenade suddenly ends, would I go into the sea?* I then realised that as the hand-bikes were made for adults, the brake was out of reach. I decided to crash-land into a lamp-post, one fitted with a wire mesh basket. My parents weren't happy with my actions. Fortunately, the hand-bike, lamp-post and wire basket survived. I was told to go slow or not at all. But the holiday was a great success and we all felt better for the break.

At home, we waved to the train drivers as they passed by the bottom of our garden. One day I sat in my wheelchair holding a bowl while my mother did some fruit picking, and it started to rain. My mother hesitated – should she take the fruit first, or me? An engine driver was shunting his train along the track and shouted 'Take the fruit! She won't melt!!' and disappeared down the line in the train. With that, my mother scarpered up the path with the fruit.

Someone asked my father to do a carpentry job, and my father agreed, as long as the wood was provided. My mother and I returned from shopping to see a policeman standing outside our front door. The policeman said that he'd been informed that we had railway wood on our property. When my mother opened the front door there was indeed a pile of wood in the hallway. The wood for the job had been pushed through the letterbox and was stamped British Rail. Although my father was innocent, he had to go to court and received a month's suspension from work.

CHAPTER 21

GOING TO SCHOOL

In the autumn of 1959, the Local Authorities informed us of a local school willing to accept me. It was a major breakthrough for my parents, who had constantly pressurised them. I could attend St John's School. I was in the last year of Junior School.

It was a small and rather old school, built on one level with just three classrooms. There were two school years in each classroom, one year on the left and the other year on the right. There was a small playground. The toilet block was at the opposite end of the playground, whitewashed and almost open to the elements. That was it. There were two steps at the entrance but in the playground there was an entrance with just one step, which I used.

We didn't own a car and I had no way of getting to school, so the Local authorities organised a school taxi. My parents upgraded the wheelchair to a folding one which went in the boot of the car. Even getting in a car for the first time was an adventure.

I couldn't wait!

It was great to be among other children again and they had no difficulty accepting me. It was usually the adults who had a problem.

I had missed all the education that children between five and ten had. My learning was very basic; my only knowledge of the world and geography was looking at an atlas. The class did listen to the same history radio sessions along with textbooks with the series. The headmistress was very hot on spelling; we were given a weekly list of words to learn. We all had to visit the Headmistress' office every week for a spelling test. The office was down two steps, but I insisted that I manage.

The playground was too small for P.E. so we used the nearby park, called *French Weir*. To get onto the path which led to the park, everyone had to climb over a knee-high wall. Undeterred, the teachers hauled me over the wall, then the wheelchair, and off we went. I sat and watched the children run around. I longed to join them, to be included. It was so hard for me to sit there and watch other children be active.

My tenth birthday was in November. Everyone celebrated their birthday at school. Each child was allowed to go to the front of the class to show their cards and one present, and we sang *Happy Birthday*! I proudly showed my cards and present while the class sang Happy Birthday to me.

I always sat at the front of the class in my wheelchair near the old coal-burning stove, which supplied heat to the large old fashioned radiators. I don't know if the floor was uneven, but whenever I walked near it I always overbalanced right by the stove. I'd reach out to grab something to stop me falling, and it was often the stove, and could hear my skin singe as I tried to save myself.

A teacher read to us from The Lion, the Witch and the Wardrobe. I listened in awe. I could believe I was there in the book. I'd never been interested in reading, and at ten years old I'd still never read a book. I wondered if maybe books could be fun.

We all attended St John's Church every Wednesday morning, and the vicar taught us religious education at school. We often used the church hall if there was a sudden gas leak from the adjacent Gas works or if the school flooded, it being near the river.

One day I was waiting in the playground for a taxi to take me home. I slipped on the wet step in the rain and fell flat on my face. The taxi man picked me up and I saw blood. My teeth had made a large gash in my mouth. There was blood on my coat and dress.

The taxi man helped me out of the taxi at home. As my mother came towards me, I shouted '*Don't you touch me, I want my dad!*' She looked stunned as I walked indoors. I hadn't planned to say that, it'd just come out. My mother and I hadn't become any closer. I'd said similar words three years earlier. The one thing I needed, love and affection, she seemed unable to give.

I kept my mouth firmly closed while I waited for my father to come home from work. There was no way of getting me to a hospital and they said the gash would heal. I had to drink through a straw and eat soft food. I'd worn braces on my teeth for two years and had just had them removed. I later found that the bang to my teeth had made my teeth crooked again.

When I began the school year in the September, I thought I would be there for the whole year but, within a few months, everything changed.

CHAPTER 22

RETURN TO HOSPITAL

Early in the New Year of 1960, I had my regular appointment with my consultant in Bath. He was still concerned about my spine curvature.

The consultant gave my parents two choices: I could have a spine operation to stop the curvature. I would need to lie on my back in plaster for six to nine months; or I could try a new type of brace, called a Milwaukee brace. This meant wearing a similar leather brace but with an iron rod up the front connected to a chin piece and a back rod connected to a support at the back of the head. The chin piece and the head support are then strapped together to help keep my back straight. I needed to wear this until I'd finished growing.

My parents wondered if a long time on my back could affect my walking, so they decided to try the Milwaukee spinal brace. The consultant explained that I wouldn't be able to move my head in any direction. Neither could I look down to see where I was walking, nor look at my lap if I was sitting down. He added that in order for me to return home, he considered our current house with the steep step into most rooms to be unsuitable. My parents needed to think about moving to a more accessible house or bungalow.

After more discussion, the consultant agreed that I could come into hospital for the new brace to be made, and then stay in hospital until my parents had found a more suitable property.

In March, I packed my bag for another trip to the Children's Ward. Although I never minded going into hospital, now that I was at school the hospital wasn't so important to me. I could do more and had got used to home life.

The brace was made and fitted. I had to get used to not being able to move my head in any direction but forward. I couldn't look down at all. I couldn't see what I was eating and anything that fell into my lap was lost. I found schoolwork hard to do: I couldn't see any school books that were placed on the table. If I held a book for long, my arms ached. It was a lot harder than I imagined it would be.

My parents frantically searched for a more accessible property, but there were none. Disabled people didn't have to be considered, as most of them still lived in special homes. Every property my parents looked at presented some kind of major problem. Eventually my parents found a builder who was beginning a new development of bungalows in Trull, close to Taunton. My parents explained the problem to the builder. He agreed to make some modifications on a specific bungalow for us. The bathroom, kitchen and hallway were all made larger so that I could move around in my wheelchair if necessary. Then we had to wait for the bungalow to be built.

Once the brace was made, I just had to wait until I could come home, wherever that might be. I became bored. At ten years old I was now one of the oldest patients in the ward. I was so glad that Pauline was with me in there. The school lessons were still the same and I understood them more now.

There were two girls I especially remember. One girl arrived from a boarding school, her parents were working abroad. She'd begun to lose the use of a leg and used crutches, then she became weaker over a short space of time. The doctors couldn't work out what was happening. The parents flew back home to be with their daughter. As soon as they started visiting, the girl started to improve and was soon walking again. The doctors put it down to stress. The girl walked out and flew abroad with her parents.

Another older girl was put in the bed next to me; they thought I was old enough to keep an eye on her. She had a learning disability. In those days, most girls with that kind of condition stayed in a special home, and they weren't equipped for a life outside. I don't remember why she was in hospital, but she made every attempt to get out of bed whenever possible. She also ate anything within reach. I watched her eat a banana with the skin. Sometimes a vicar came round with some song books and we had a short service. Before I realised it, he'd handed a book to this girl, who tore out the pages and started eating them. The vicar looked aghast. Thank goodness times have changed and now anyone with a learning disability can be a valued member of the community.

An Occupational Therapist said I was welcome to visit their department to see the various crafts they offered. Sister Mumford gave me permission to make my own way in my wheelchair along the corridor to get involved after school. It was full of different crafts. The role of the Occupational Therapists was very different back then; they concentrated on keeping hospital patients busy and improving their skills. I wanted to try everything. I made a tray using cane and a rope stool. One day they gave me a pattern and felt, to make a Bambi. She showed me how to sew the pieces together and what stitches to use. I'd never sewn before and I loved it. I asked for more patterns and couldn't wait for school to end so that I could race down the corridor to sew. My love of sewing had started.

The months went by. Summer came, and then autumn. Once again, my schoolwork was suffering. I didn't go back to school during that school year.

My parents and Stuart moved into the new bungalow on 29th September. I still couldn't come home, as the paths and road weren't finished. My parents walked across boards to get indoors. I eventually went home in November. I'd spent nearly ten months in hospital.

CHAPTER 23

ANOTHER NEW HOME

For the second time in my young life, I had to enter a place called home with no idea of what it might look like. My parents were proud of their achievement and I could see that they wanted praise from me as well.

I came home just in time for my eleventh birthday. As Christmas was approaching, I noticed my father disappear into their bedroom regularly, and he would start singing. My father couldn't sing, and so I found this most odd. All was revealed on Christmas Day when I was given a clock in a case with a ballerina underneath. Every hour the tune started and the ballerina twirled around. I was fascinated by it and still have it, though unfortunately it's not working now.

My bedroom window looked over the front garden, and my room had been specially prepared for me. The bed was in the middle of the room, with a small cupboard beside and a wardrobe along one wall. I smiled and said thank you. Stuart had the third bedroom which was much smaller. It was lovely to be on one level and to walk into my bedroom whenever I wanted. I noticed there was nowhere for me to sit in my bedroom, and no room for my wheelchair. I found it hard to sit on my bed or ordinary chairs; I asked if I could sit in my room, and was told I could use the settee in the lounge. After being in a ward of thirty children, I longed for some privacy, but didn't want to sound ungrateful. My mother insisted that I keep my door open at all times. She wanted to check on me.

My parents said that although there was more room in the bungalow, the wheelchair had to stay folded up in the hall by the front door. I could use the wheelchair for after baths to get from the bath to my bed, and to use when I went outside. I needed to keep walking to achieve independence.

I don't think anyone really realised what a struggle it was to constantly walk. My new brace made it harder. My brace and callipers rubbed and it was so uncomfortable. I'd stayed in my wheelchair most of the time in the hospital, it was so quick and easy to get around and do things. I felt more independent using my wheelchair and I didn't get so tired.

We now lived nearly two miles outside of Taunton, and up a hill. No-one seemed to think it was an issue except me. We didn't have a car, and there was no accessible transport, so I was stuck at home. There were no more family outings, no more visits to town. The bungalow had to be my world.

My father went to work on a motor-scooter, Stuart used a bicycle and my mother caught the bus. I just sat on the same settee and looked out of the window at the bungalow opposite. I felt so isolated. I knew they meant well, but I wanted so much to go out and have fun instead of being on my own again. If I said anything negative, I was reminded just how much time, money and effort they had spent to enable me to come home. Years later my mother said she was glad we'd moved as no-one locally would know that she was our stepmother; and yet it always seemed to be my fault if anything happened.

It was hard to adjust to family life again after so long in hospital. The dynamics of our family had changed again while I'd been away, with us each leading a separate life. Still no more family outings to bring us together. Stuart was in his last year at school. He often cycled into town to meet up with friends, Scouts and a youth club. My mother said she was no longer willing to push me anywhere in my wheelchair. She said that she had done enough of that from our house in town. If I wanted to go anywhere, then it was up to my father to push me there; so my father pushed me to Guides and Stuart pushed me to Sunday School.

I showed my mother the Bambi I had made in hospital, and asked if she could buy me a pattern and some felt. She came home with a pattern for a small donkey and some grey felt. I sat on my own for hours making lots of donkeys. I sold them for pocket money.

One day, I noticed an Enid Blyton book about the Famous Five. I picked it up and opened it. I read the first page and turned it over. I turned another page and got into the story. I was 10 and was finally reading my first book.

Dressmaking was even more stressful. My new brace with the rod extensions meant that nothing fitted me. My mother still made my clothes and had to alter any pattern, and I had to rely on her choice of material as I couldn't get into town. The dresses were all to the same design and tended to be big and baggy. I found it difficult to stand still for fittings. I longed to choose my own dress, and I didn't see what other children wore. We were often in nighties on the ward, or we were in school uniform or Guide uniform.

I should have left the Junior School in the July to move up to Secondary School. The Local Authorities agreed that I could have another year with the juniors to try to catch up with my schoolwork. In the January, I started school again. I had to sit my eleven-plus exam. I heard my parents say that with my lack of education, I wouldn't pass, so I didn't bother. The weather was horrible that day and I spent most of the time looking out of the window. Of course, I failed. The next problem was to find an accessible Secondary School. The Local Authority still said they wanted me to go away to school. My parents said 'No'.

I found school work even more difficult because I couldn't look down to do any writing. My father designed a tray to fit across my wheelchair with a board made at an angle so that I could place my work on it. The problem was that if I pressed too much the board collapsed. My arms soon ached from writing high-up. The pen didn't always work if it wasn't pointing at the right angle. The board was kept at school, so I couldn't use it at home.

In the new year our neighbours moved in, and Lynne and Phillip lived next door. They were younger than me and we played games together on our driveway. Other children from around the cul-de-sac often joined in. Sometimes I fell over and they rushed to find an adult who could stand me up.

I'd expressed a wish to play the piano and my parents managed to find an old piano which they put in the lounge. I had a retired piano teacher to tutor me and I soon realised that it wasn't as easy as I'd thought. My parents said I had made a commitment and needed to continue.

CHAPTER 24

SECONDARY SCHOOL

I started my first term at Askwith Secondary School in South Street the following September. It was a small school with about two hundred pupils and the headmaster was happy to accept me. It was a compact building, all on one level.

There was a small hall with four classrooms leading off, plus two more classrooms just along the corridor, outside the hall. The English, Maths, Cookery and Science classes were held in mobile huts spaced around the playground. Once again, the toilets were in a block at the far side of the playground, painted with whitewash.

It was a mixed school. The small hall was used for assembly each morning, lessons and school dinners. It was a tight squeeze and some children had to eat in the adjoining classrooms as we only had one sitting. We had no uniform, a lot of parents said they couldn't afford it. Some of the lads often got into trouble with the police, who seemed to visit the school regularly. I can remember one day when a father came to assembly and lifted the headmaster off the floor, demanding that his son not be given detention anymore.

Because I'd missed a lot of education, I really struggled with the schoolwork. I hadn't realised just how much I'd missed as I tried so hard to understand. I'd just read my first book, the Enid Blyton book, and in English we were given a book to read, called The Cruel Sea by Nicholas Monsarrat. It follows the lives of a group of Royal Navy sailors fighting the Battle of the Atlantic during the Second World War. I struggled from the beginning.

I sat at the back of the class in my wheelchair, by choice. I hoped that by doing this the teacher wouldn't pick on me to answer a question. The problem was that from the back of the class I couldn't see the blackboard very well, so my schoolwork suffered even more. I used the board and stand my father had made to hide behind. Maths was my worst subject. I only knew the basics. I had never done fractions, percentages, or algebra. As the maths sessions got more complex, I was completely left behind. I copied other classmates' work when I could.

Our classroom doubled as the needlework room and although I loved sewing, I hated needlework at school. Our first project was to make a sewing bag. I sewed as slowly as I could. Then we had to make an apron. The girls surged ahead, starting to use patterns and make clothes. Girls did more sewing in those days as it was cheaper, and clothes were limited to buy. The sewing machines were treadle types, used by the feet, so there was no way I could use one. The teacher never discussed with me what the options might be or how I could progress. I often undid sewing so that I did the same amount again the next time. Sewing became stressful for me at school, which was a shame, as it was the only thing I felt good at and enjoyed.

I soon settled into school routine and my classmates were happy to push me around. We often played a game where I sat in my wheelchair holding onto my sticks which I held in front of me, while the girls and lads would race around the playground with me like a chariot in full pursuit. Sometimes my wheelchair turned over as we sped around corners too quickly, but I was never hurt.

We messed around in class at any opportunity. As we walked into our geography lesson once, the boys picked up and hid the teacher's glasses. They got handed around as the teacher accused different children. As we left the classroom, someone sneaked the glasses back on the front desk.

We had religious education in the hall. That was a different teacher, another one we could easily play up. Children always seem to know what they can get away with.

Music lessons were the worst. I can't remember ever learning anything. The teacher wandered around the classroom with two rulers tied together ready to flick at us if we dared to play up. By the end of each session there were often quite a few boys standing with their hands on their heads. We had homework to do. When it was handed back, there were remarks such as:

'Write: 'I must dot my i a hundred times', or 'I must dash my t a hundred times'.

I never knew what this was meant to achieve, but as none of us wanted the ruler treatment, we didn't argue.

At one music lesson, we had the cookery teacher because the music teacher was ill. She played the piano and we all sang but afterwards she kept on playing. One of the pupils went to tell the headmaster. He came along and ushered us out of the classroom quietly. We never saw the cookery teacher again; we were told that she'd suffered a nervous breakdown.

We had eye tests from time to time. All the children queued for the test, and when it was my turn to read the letters, I had to admit that the letters were blurred, and I couldn't tell what they were. The nurse looked puzzled and then said 'It's probably the angle of your brace,' and signalled for me to leave, and another child to come. The real problem was that I was quite short-sighted. No-one had paid much attention to my eyesight, and of course, my parents relied on the school tests.

I had never queried my eyesight. I was used to seeing everything slightly blurred, so I thought that was normal; though I did wonder why I could never read the blackboard and all the other children could.

Because the nurse had put my blurred vision down to the tilt of my head, I had to spend the whole of my school life being short-sighted, with no glasses. I would've benefitted so much more if I'd been given glasses; they would have helped me with my schoolwork and life in general. It wasn't until the last term at secondary school when my short-sightedness came to light.

I was given homework for the first time. My tray and board stayed at school, which meant I didn't have anything to use at home. I found that if I stood leaning against a high cupboard in my bedroom I could bend over slightly and actually see my homework books. This meant that all my homework was done standing up. As I grew older, I would stand for hours in this way. My legs ached and my callipers pinched me, but I never said anything. I didn't know another option. My parents never said anything, and I found it hard to concentrate. I wonder how many other children stood for hours to do their homework?

At parents evenings, and the end of term report on my progress, my parents were told I could do better and should read more. The English teacher asked me to run a Book Club. I handed around the booklist but many children didn't have the money for books, so I didn't do much. I did buy a few books for myself, but then lost interest.

We had a Penny Bank at school. Every Friday we could invest any spare money. My mother gave me some money to put in the bank. Instead of putting it in the bank, it gave me the chance to go with some of the other children to a local sweetshop and buy sweets. That was fun, as we chose our sweets from the big jars. It was one of the very few shops I went into. We always shared our sweets around.

We had swimming lessons at the local pool. I was keen to take part even though I couldn't swim. The teachers said I could join in but they didn't have the time to help me get ready. My mother agreed to come and help me get changed.

When we turned up at the pool, the staff told us to go to the back entrance to avoid the steps. Then came the next problem: the girls changing rooms weren't accessible. They pondered as to where we could go, and then someone said 'There's the boiler room,' so that's where I got changed. Everything stuck to us with the heat and we both emerged the colour of beetroot.

Once in the water, I was free again. To begin with, I swam using a ring. One day I fell out of the ring and began slipping under the water. I tried hard with my breaststrokes and to my surprise found myself swimming. I could swim!

At Christmas, the school announced we could have a treat. We all walked through town to the cinema to see a film. It was a black and white comedy film called A Stitch in Time starring Norman Wisdom. It was so funny. Once again, I had trouble getting into a seat but managed with help from the teachers.

In May of 1962, the whole school went to the Bath and West Show. Our transport turned out to be open-topped farm lorries. We all squeezed on, waving at passers-by in excitement as we trundled along. I was having so much fun.

Life was so much better.

CHAPTER 25

Young Adult Ward

Soon after starting my first year at Secondary School, another hospital visit was required. I had grown out of my brace and callipers.

This time I was directed towards the Young Adult Ward. I was a little more apprehensive as I was shown my bed and said goodbye to my parents. The ward consisted of girls in their teens, and I was twelve years old. Then I spotted Pauline, she had been moved as well. We were always pleased to meet up again. It helped so much having Pauline around. She was my link, even though we never corresponded between visits.

Sister Bray suddenly burst through the doors of the ward and issued orders like a Sergeant Major. She was fairly short and well-built, and her voice boomed around the ward. She wasn't going to stand for any nonsense. The Sister in the Children's Ward had been strict, but had a motherly smile. This wasn't going to happen here. You either did as you were told, or were reported. There were still no curtains around the bed, and no television.

When I first entered the Children's Ward in 1955, most of the children were long-stay patients as a result of serious illnesses, such as polio. Vaccinations and better health care meant that fewer children were becoming disabled now. The hospital system had changed as a result.

The hospital specialised in orthopaedics. Girls entered to have their operation or treatment and were soon out again with crutches. Pauline and I were the only two girls who had seen so much hospital life.

There were no school lessons in this ward. Girls could leave school at 15, so lessons weren't appropriate. Anyone still at school had to bring their own books and study by themselves. On future visits, I did take schoolwork with me but found it hard to concentrate and nothing much got done.

I had regular visits to the appliance centre for my new brace and callipers. I had to be strung-up between two poles and stretched twice. Once, to make a Plaster of Paris mould for my new leather brace, and another time for a new plaster bed to sleep in. The leather brace then had to be trimmed into shape so as not to dig in and rub me. It was a slow process. Not enough leather cut back and it dug into me, too much cut off rendered the brace useless. I fastened the brace with Velcro straps. Steel supports were fitted to support my chin and the back of my head in an attempt to stretch my spine as I grew. When I wasn't having a fitting, I spent most of my time in bed. I was allowed to sit up with a back rest. I had a large wire cradle to stop the bedclothes pushing on my feet.

I soon made friends. One of the girls called me Bobtail, as when my name was called I popped up over the foot cradle. Soon the other two girls were named Rag and Tag, after the television series. We had such fun together.

One girl had been given a wind-up portable record player, with some records, by her parents. If Sister was off duty we got away with playing some of the records.

We were always woken around 6.00 a.m. and then had to wait for the day staff to arrive for breakfast. One morning I asked if I could borrow the record player and started to play some records. Gradually, the level of the noise increased as we all sang and moved to the music. It was like a mini disco at 7.30 in the morning. I put on the record Drink Up Thee Cider by the Wurzels, and I was busy singing away when I realised that I was the only girl singing. I slowly turned around to face Sister Bray, who had come on duty, her face as red as a beetroot. She was looming over me, and furious. She snatched away the record player, which was immediately confiscated, and she marched from the ward. There was now complete silence. I apologised to the girl who owned the record player. She said that if we couldn't play it, what was the point of having it in the hospital anyway?

The next time my parents came to visit me, Sister Bray stomped into the ward and said in a loud voice, 'Mr and Mrs Sandford, I'd like to see you in my office, please,' and marched out. My father leant forward and said 'What have you done now?' I heard my mother chuckle. She poked my father and said, 'Come on Len, let's go for our next lecture.' They composed themselves and walked into the Sister's office. They were so used to this now I think they just listened quietly. I don't think I was a naughty child, just mischievous and letting off steam.

I was in hospital for six weeks. I'd already missed so much education and now I was missing lessons in the Senior School. Whenever I went back to school, the lessons had moved on to other subjects. I was always being left behind.

There was no help or assistance for a disabled child at school as there is now. The Local Authority said if a disabled child needed help, then they should be in a special school. I heard that the education at a special school was basic. The opinion was that there was no need to educate disabled children: they were young people who'd stay in care all their lives.

Luckily for me, my mother had a strong personality; she wasn't going to let the Local Authority tell her and my father what should be done. She could be called a pioneer for disabled rights. Someone had to stick-up for us.

CHAPTER 26

Pathfinders Camp

I wanted to go camping with my Guide Company, but nothing was accessible. Someone mentioned Pathfinders Camp on Woodlarks Campsite near Farnham, Surrey, *which is* geared for disabled people. Pathfinders Camp was then a Guide Camp, so it was ideal for me.

I was really excited as we travelled by train so that I could stay for the week. Two helpers assisted me settling into our tent. This was a whole new experience for me and I was revelling in the company and the different activities. I could join in everything, even the chores! No sitting on the sidelines looking on. I wanted to try everything.

It was the first time I'd mixed with other disabled people, and soon made friends. It felt good to be on equal terms.

We ate our meals outside sitting on groundsheets, or hiked into the woods to cook sausages and dampers (flour and water mixed, then wrapped around a stick and held over the fire). Filled with jam, they were just about edible. We collected the wood, lit the fires and helped to cook the food.

On sports day we went charging around the campsite in our wheelchairs trying to beat the other patrols. We had obstacle courses; we carried water over the bumps in the ground, ate donuts off string and ended up exhausted and laughing.

We had swimming galas, involving those girls who could not swim by keeping them busy. We had to carry a candle or a plate with the crackers across the pool. There was often a dressing-up race.

In the afternoons, we could swim in the heated outdoor swimming pool, try archery, go on the aerial runway: a chair attached by a pulley, flying across the woods, or try various crafts. There was so much to do.

On Wednesdays, we dressed in our Guide uniforms and were loaded onto coaches for an outing. Over the years, we went to many places, but I always enjoyed a trip on the River Thames. We sang campfire songs on the return journey. We often bought some snacks and had a midnight feast in our tent at night.

In the evenings, we gathered around a large campfire and sang campfire songs, linking arms with our new friends, with a starlit sky above us. We listened to stories and performed funny stunts. A small group of us went into the woods at night to see a fox's hole and maybe a fox. I had to be carried, someone tripped in the dark and we ended up in a heap trying to find our torches. No hope of seeing a fox, but we did laugh.

One evening it was pouring with rain and we had to cross some ground to our tent. My helper said 'Hang on, and I'll run with you.' We headed off at a great speed in the dark. Suddenly we came to a full stop as we'd hit something. It was the flagpole. I'd left my wheelchair, jolted-out, and found myself wrapped around the flagpole, then slid down and back into my wheelchair, shaken but not hurt. We ran on to our tent, giggling away. Fortunately, the flagpole survived.

There are woods around the campsite with accessible paths and I loved wandering through them; woods had been out of reach for me. I stayed silent, hoping to see wildlife, and was rewarded with sightings of a deer on many occasions.

Towards the end of my week at camp, I was horrified to see my parents walking up the drive one day. They'd come to see if I was alright. I decided they weren't going to spoil my fun, and I ignored them. I think they left fairly soon, realising that I was fine.

The end of the first week came all too soon, it was hard to say goodbye. I'd made so many friends and there was so much I could do. I didn't want to go home. It was like having a new family. I couldn't wait to go back again, and counted the months until the time came again.

Pathfinders Camp definitely changed my life, and I have so many life-long friends from Camp. Over the years we have met between Camp and have been on holidays together and enjoyed weekends away in London. I have stayed with friends and watched their children grow.

We held Camp Reunions at Easter, staying in various hotels around the country. We explored the countryside, had boat trips and disappeared into caves. We went to a fair, and I had my first trip as a passenger in a bumper car. Every time someone hit our car, I shot off the seat into the foot well, where I eventually stayed, much to the amusement of onlookers. I didn't realise how much other people used the strength in their legs to keep them on the seat.

Some of us had the chance to go for a speedboat ride. As the boat took off, so did I. Everyone had to hang on to me to stop me bouncing off the seat.

One day, when we were eating our lunch at Portland Bill on the Isle of Portland, someone said: 'Does anyone want to climb the lighthouse?'

'Oh – I do!' I said, without thinking. Climbing steps and stairs had always been a challenge, and now I had agreed to try and climb really steep winding stairs to the top of the lighthouse, 153 steps in all. Walking with callipers meant they did not bend at the knee unless I sat down.

'Right!' said Malc and Stan, wondering how on earth we were going to achieve this. I had to lean right over so that Malc could lift my straight leg up a step. Stan went in front to heave me up a step while Malc pushed from behind. Progress was slow. There was no room for anyone else to overtake us, going up or coming down, it was so narrow. Eventually we reached the top. I think I said something like: 'It's not as high up as I thought.' The two men raised their eyebrows.

It felt to me as though I'd climbed Mount Everest with the amount of effort we'd put into the climb. Gravity helped us as we came back down. It was so exciting to have climbed a lighthouse!

As an adult I helped to run the Camp, assisting with activities along with the friends I had made over the years. We worked together to pass on the same experience and knowledge that had been passed on to us.

Pathfinders is still a very successful camp. Campers and helpers are keen to camp and enjoy the experience together. Camp life and the friends I made helped me so much. I hope it will be the same for the campers and helpers who come to camp now and in the future.

CHAPTER 27

Isolated

After Christmas and into the new year of 1963, it snowed heavily, turning our cul-de-sac into a white wilderness. The snow lay nearly two feet thick and the drifts even higher. The milkman left milk by the main road, and everyone had to plough through snow to get any provisions and into town.

There was no way I could go anywhere. I watched from the window as my father and Stuart trudged up the road in their wellington boots. I couldn't get to school. The snowy weather continued through January and most of February, so I missed the first two months of schooling. My parents had insisted on having heating installed when the bungalow was built, out of the norm in those days; so I kept warm.

In the mornings, my mother listened to Housewife's Choice on the radio, often humming to the tunes as she worked. I decided to send in a song request for her birthday in February. I carefully wrote a postcard, requesting anything from South Pacific as I knew this was a favourite. I put it in an envelope and got someone to post it. I was constantly trying to please her so that she might like me.

The snow gradually melted and I started school on 25th February, which happened to be the day of my mother's birthday. My mother was hanging out the washing, a neighbour shouted over to her that the record playing on the radio was for *her*. They played I'm Gonna Wash That Man Right Outta My Hair. Not quite the song I would've chosen. Instead of thanking me, she found it funny. She joked with my father about the title of the song.

We had a new headmaster and a new set of rules. Uniform was compulsory. He started a school youth club, and he asked me if I'd like to go, and I told him that I had no transport. He said he'd drive out to pick me up every week; I wanted to take my wheelchair with me but my parents said no, it was a hassle just for a couple of hours. I couldn't sit on an ordinary chair without falling off, so I stood the entire evening. I didn't really know how to socialise; I took myself to a corner of the hall and watched, trying to make it look as though I was having a good time.

Now and again someone came up to me and asked me if I was alright, and I said 'I'm fine'. I wasn't, I felt just as lonely watching other children have a good time. They wandered around in groups drinking squash and dancing or playing table tennis.

The wooden floor was polished and I found it incredibly slippery. I was scared of falling. In wet weather, the wet floor became even more treacherous for me. I had to decline a drink, I hated the thought of trying to negotiate my way across the playground in the dark to reach the toilets. I told my parents I wanted to stop going, but they said I should be grateful the headmaster wanted to help me. I asked if I could take my wheelchair, and the answer, again, was no.

I arrived at school one morning to discover I had left the wheelchair at home. I couldn't manage without it, so the headmaster drove to our home to fetch it. My mother was out. He noticed the top kitchen window was open, so he put the dustbin under the window and climbed onto it, reached to open the bigger window, climbed in and then walked out of the front door with my wheelchair.

My parents decided that I should start confirmation classes at the local vicarage. My father pushed me there in the evenings. I didn't really understand any of it and so, as in school, I stayed quiet. This way people thought I was fine. If I said anything, I might give myself away.

I wasn't sure about religion or even God. I didn't enjoy going to church, but had no choice. I was dressed in white to become confirmed. My parents were proud of watching me receive my first and only communion. After that, I said 'Never again!' and was just glad it was all over. They could be proud of Stuart, he was training to become a Sunday School teacher.

A young girl, about eighteen, asked if she could come and help me for a day towards a project. We played games and went for a stroll in my wheelchair, and I was on a high. I asked if she could come again. On her way out, I heard my mother say, 'I expect she has asked you to come again. Don't worry about that, she'll be fine.'

Having her company had shown me what life could be like if I had young people around me. Why didn't my mother understand that?

I enjoyed school but spent the weekends on my own in the lounge or standing up doing homework. There was no way I could go into town or meet up with my classmates. I listened to the other girls at school talking about shopping trips, going to discos, finding boyfriends. It sounded like another world, one I couldn't be part of. I felt sad and also angry at not being able to take part in everyday life. *How was it that so many other young people could go out and enjoy life, while I spent so much time on my own?* I couldn't talk to my parents, they just said I was ungrateful. Stuart and I didn't say much to each other. Four years is quite a wide gap. I was twelve and he was sixteen, he had already left school and was working in County Hall.

I couldn't let other people see how I felt. They expected me to be always smiling, so I did when in company. My true feelings were kept hidden. It seemed that if you weren't disabled you could be sad and be comforted. If you had a disability and looked sad or angry, you were either ungrateful or you had a chip on your shoulder.

I felt excluded from a society who didn't seem to care that most disabled people were shut away. There were so many places still inaccessible even if I did go out. Some disabled people were beginning to fight for the right to be accepted in society. It was a slow and uphill struggle.

CHAPTER 28

THREE PHRASES

I was often scared of my mother. If she approached, I would back away if I could; it was impossible to know what was about to happen. I seemed to be so often in the wrong. If I thought she was going to hit me, I would flinch, waiting for it to happen, as I was powerless to run away. Sometimes she just wanted to talk to me, but I had that wary look about me, which probably made her angry.

Her mood could change in an instant. I don't think she had any idea how she was making me feel. My father and Stuart often received the sharp end of her tongue too. I wished I was brave enough to say that I was afraid, but when you are young and scared you don't have the confidence to say anything.

My mother had three phrases she regularly used to keep us in order. The first one was 'Spare the rod and spoil the child'. She thought there was no harm in giving me a slap across the face if she thought I deserved it. The problem was I never knew when it was going to happen. I never knew what I had said or done wrong. My mother had a quick temper; she would suddenly march across the room, slap me across the face and quickly disappear. I just wished she would explain what the problem was and give me a chance to apologise, but it never happened. I didn't get slapped often, but always had to be wary if my mother was near me, just in case. I was always on my own when she did this. I never knew if Stuart received the same treatment as I never mentioned it to anyone. I don't think my father ever knew.

I remember standing in the kitchen leaning against the wall by the larder, having a conversation with my mother, who was at the sink. Suddenly, my mother turned and sped towards me; I tried to think what I'd said to upset her as I braced myself for the coming slap. I could never run away. Instead, my mother picked something up from the larder and marched back to the sink. My body shook as I realised it was a false alarm. I would've sunk to the floor except my callipers were holding me up. It was some minutes before I could move.

I remember one morning in particular. Stuart and I were in the kitchen. I was getting ready for school and Stuart was leaving for work. My mother was cutting bread and angry about something. She suddenly turned around and lashed out but she forgot she had a breadknife in her hand. The blade of the knife hit my brother on the shoulder and I saw blood running down his arm. I could see by the look on her face that she was as horrified as we were. There was a stunned silence.

Stuart grabbed his jacket, rushed out to his bike and cycled to work. My school transport arrived and I quickly left. The incident was never mentioned, but later I found out that Stuart had needed stitches. My mother said that as a child her grandmother would roll up a newspaper to hit her on the legs if she did anything wrong. She had constant arguments with her own father, who also had a quick temper. She came from an era where everyone was expected to work hard to help the family.

Another phrase was 'My bark is worse than my bite'. My mother often said it jokingly when in company. She said, 'Rita knows my bark is worse than my bite,' except I *didn't* know. I was meant to smile or laugh but I didn't; to me her bark was as bad as her bite. I think she meant me not to take to heart everything she said, but I did. I never heard her say anything nice unless we were in company. She often said 'I'm teaching Rita to stand up for herself,' but I had no confidence whatsoever. How could I, when everything I did was wrong?

'Children are to be seen and not heard.' She expected children to be obedient. We had to be at the kitchen table well before mealtimes so as not to be in the way, and to be quiet. When we had visitors, I was expected to keep quiet and my mother quite happily talked about me while I sat there. Everyone looked at me and nodded. I was so used to this I came to rely on my mother to do all the socialising.

On one occasion, my mother left me alone with visitors while she went to make some tea. I panicked... *they might try to talk to me!* What would I say? I fled the room and hid until I heard my mother talking again. As I came back into the room the visitors gave me a funny look, but my mother didn't notice. She was in full flow again; I had no worries about having to speak. I just sat on the settee and looked out of the window. I didn't know how to socialise with adults. My teachers had the same problem with me at school. I listened to them but they rarely got an answer.

My mother laughed and joked when she was in company. Why was she never like that with us, I wondered?

Many years later, my mother spoke about her father. Apparently, he could laugh and joke with friends but was so harsh and strict at home.

It seemed to me that father and daughter were very alike.

I never saw my mother happy, I don't know why, but it affected all of us. Nothing we ever did was right. I crept around the place trying to be invisible. Even when she gave me a birthday card to sign, she expected me to make a mistake, so I often did. Even now, I have to take a deep breath to sign a card, and still make mistakes. One day while I was standing in my bedroom doing my homework, my mother appeared at the bedroom door and said 'If it hadn't been for you, your father and I could've been happy.' With that, she disappeared. What had I done to make her so unhappy?

My father was always busy, either at work, in the garden or in the garage using his skills as a carpenter. He didn't want to be part of any arguments and I'm sure he just stayed out of the way for that reason. But he didn't always help the situation. When my father arrived home from work, my mother would pounce on him, complaining about her day, often saying that she wasn't well. My father would get out his diary and open it to the date, with pen poised, he'd ask: 'And what is wrong with you today?' That infuriated my mother.

Consequently, I felt stuck in the middle.

I just wished I could escape for a while, go for a walk, meet with friends, but I couldn't. I felt trapped in a situation I couldn't change.

Over time, heated arguments materialised between my parents, usually after I went to bed. I never knew what they were about. Twice my mother packed her bags and left. My father went after her and brought her home, full of regret.

He still needed her. One day they had an argument in the kitchen. I tried to get between them to stop them. One of them accidentally hit me and sent me flying across the kitchen. I landed in a heap beside the fridge. They looked at me horrified. It stopped the fight.

We never did anything together as a family, no social outings to draw us together. There was no accessible transport for me to help us get out and visit places. We were just four people trying to cope. Having spent so much time away from home, I had no real knowledge about family life. I believed that parents had to have children whether they wanted them or not. Surely if parents had a choice, they'd only have children if they wanted them? I didn't feel wanted.

No-one in our family shared any affection. I saw my parents as people I had to be with. I had no choice. If someone had said to me that I needed to leave my parents forever, I'd have just packed my bags and said goodbye. Does that make me a bad person? Who is there to blame?

Maybe no-one is. We're all affected by our past experiences, like it or not.

CHAPTER 29

KITCHEN AND BISCUIT ETIQUETTE

The kitchen was my mother's domain. I rarely ventured into it unless asked, as I was usually in the way. I often stayed by the hallway entrance to the kitchen to watch, or to ask her something.

We had breakfast, lunch and evening meal during the week, and breakfast, dinner and tea at weekends. My parents didn't ever consider sitting down mid-morning or afternoon for a break and a drink; you just didn't do that in those days, they were far too busy. It didn't dawn on me to ask for anything between meals, and knew I would've been refused anyway. There was no need, and I was never hungry.

But the kitchen did hold a kind of fascination for me, partly because it was off-limits. Sometimes when my mother said she was going to the village stores or post office, I ventured into the kitchen to look around. I found a tin of biscuits. Who were they for, I wondered? I was never offered a biscuit. Could I have one? My heart pounded as I tried to figure out if my mother would notice. I would definitely be in trouble if she did. I took one, and disappeared into the lounge, worried that my mother might suddenly return.

After that, I kept an eye on the tin and occasionally took a biscuit. I noticed that the biscuits changed, as different ones were added. I wondered where they were going, as they were definitely not available to me.

It was a mystery.

The only time my parents stopped for a cup of tea was if friends or relations came, the biscuits put on a plate and the best china brought out. After leaving home, I sometimes called in, and my mother often made a cup of tea and the tin of biscuits came out. At last, I was officially allowed a biscuit. I found the whole thing very strange, and I smile about it now.

I could never tell them that I'd known about the biscuit tin all along.

CHAPTER 30

ANOTHER TRAGEDY

It was August 1963 and I was packing for Pathfinders Camp. I was so excited, and Susan was coming with me from the village.

Stuart was involved in a Youth Club exchange. The year before, Stuart had travelled to Holland to stay with a family. Now it was our turn to host a Dutch lad, but I would be at camp at that time.

I had a terrific time at camp, Sue and I had so much fun together. It was lovely to meet up with everyone I'd known from before. My parents had taken us to camp by train, and so I was surprised when Sue's parents arrived by car to take us home. I sat in the front revelling in the fact that I was going home in a *car*. Sue and her mother sat in the back.

I chatted away about camp, but after a while I began to notice that Sue was very quiet and just looked out of the window. As I gradually stopped talking I felt a heavy atmosphere in the car. I stayed quiet for the rest of the way home. When we arrived, my parents rushed out, thanking Sue and her parents. They were whispering. There was something wrong. What was it?

When I reached the kitchen, my parents explained that Stuart had been involved in a motor accident and had died. I was stunned and could only stare back at them. This couldn't be true; he was alive and busy with Hans when I left for camp. They were standing together by the sink and I was standing the other side of the room by the larder. I didn't know what to say. They stood still, waiting for my reaction. They didn't come any closer or try to comfort me.

Hans, the Dutch lad, had used Stuart's bike to cycle into town for a meeting. He was late coming home. Stuart had asked if he could borrow our father's bike to go and meet him. As he got to the top of the road, he saw Hans cycling up the main road, and waved. Stuart then started to cross the road by bike. A motorcyclist driving at high speed collided with him. Neither survived, and Hans saw it all happen.

Without uttering a word, I walked to my bedroom, slammed the door shut, and fell onto the bed. I didn't cry. I felt as though my world had crashed around me. Stuart and I hadn't been that close, but we were brother and sister and he had been part of our fragile family. I lay on my bed for a long time on my own, wondering what to do and how to cope. Gradually I formed a plan. I could pretend that Stuart wasn't dead, he had just gone away for a while. That way I didn't need to cry. I could pretend that it hadn't happened.

I walked into the kitchen and asked what was for tea. We sat in silence while eating, and then I went off to bed.

My parents never mentioned Stuart again. It was as though Stuart had never existed and been erased from their memories. They probably thought this was easier for me, and it was in a way, but I was deeply affected by Stuart's death, and needed their support. It just wasn't there for me.

Nowadays, people are encouraged to talk about the death of a loved one and remember them. This wasn't the case in our day: people whispered and said nothing. I was in denial, and in order to cope I opted for a 'I don't care' attitude. I think my parents believed me. It was all a front for me, I was really hurting inside. I had never grieved for my mother, who I couldn't remember, and I didn't know how to grieve for my brother.

My parents decided that I shouldn't attend the funeral. Maybe it would've been real if I'd gone. My parents, relations and friends were all trying to compose themselves, and perhaps I would've embarrassed them. I don't know. Christine came down from London with her parents Uncle Ken and Aunt Mariette, and she and I spent the afternoon with Susan in her garden. We pretended to be happy, but knew what was really happening.

Some months later, I was helping at a Christmas bazaar when a lady asked me how Stuart was. I was stunned at her question. 'He's fine,' I said, and slipped away. I couldn't say the words 'Stuart has died,' and if I did I might cry, and I couldn't let that happen. I just hadn't come to terms with Stuart's death.

I started to say I was an only child to people who didn't know; it was easier that way.

Hans came from Holland to stay for Christmas. It'd been very difficult for him, as he'd witnessed the accident and had to attend court for the inquest. He was only seventeen. We felt we had to make the effort for him over Christmas. A few years later we went to stay with his family for a holiday.

The Christmas before, Stuart had asked if I would like a record as a Christmas present and I said I would. Stuart was seventeen and owned a record player and really enjoyed the music of the 60's. It was the beginning of The Beatles and The Rolling Stones, an exciting time in the history of music.

I had no real interest in music at that time. My mother always had Radio 4 on and I went no-where to hear modern music. On Christmas Day, I had no idea who the singer or musicians were on the record, but started to thank Stuart, when our mother had a real go at Stuart for buying me a record. I should have said that he had asked me, and felt guilty afterwards. Why had I not backed up Stuart? It's these little things that I still think of. I have never been able to put it right and so the guilt, however small, stays with me.

My parents finally started to talk about Stuart and the things he did. They had each other for support, but I had no-one. I either changed the subject or walked away. My parents were always annoyed at my *don't care* attitude. If only they'd really known how I felt inside.

I have very few memories of Stuart, it all seems a blur now. Over the years I wished I'd made more of an effort for us to get to know each other. I thought we'd have a lifetime together for that. I've always felt slightly guilty to be the one still alive.

Rita and Stuart - 1954

Rita - 1954

My mother, Stuart and me taken at the top of Burrow Mump. The last photo taken before we caught polio - 1955

The first photo of me in hospital - 1956

Stuart and my father visiting me in hospital - 1956

Bath. Waiting for the Duke of Edinburgh to visit - 1956

In a new wheelchair, with Kath - 1957

Worthing Holiday. My father, Kath, Stuart and me - 1958

With Stuart at Worthing - 1958

Me with Tower of London Beefeaters - 1959

Me at Askwith School - 1964

Walking - 6 Mile Hike - 1964

Plus Ultra Award - Spain - 1964

In hospital with Pauline - 1965

Noddy Car. Ministry three-wheel fibreglass car - 1967

In garden of new bungalow - 1988

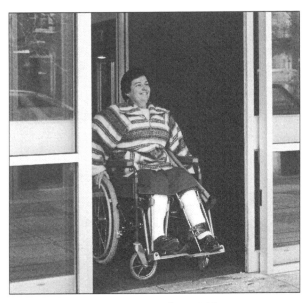

Leaving work - 1988

CHAPTER 31

SMALL COMFORT

In the New Year after Stuart's death, my parents said that I could have a dog. My mother suggested a poodle, as they shed no hair. They hoped it would be company for me. I picked out a black poodle which I named Nicky. He was adorable and as he grew older he did sit on my lap on the settee, but I felt he wasn't really my dog. He adored my father and, with his canine instincts, could always hear my father coming back from work on his Honda in the road outside, way before he was visible. He raced to the door to greet him.

My father took him for walks. Whenever I asked if I could go with him, I was always turned down; it meant my father would have to push me in my wheelchair. I had to watch out of the window as my father set off with Nicky. *Could my parents not see that I needed to get out of the bungalow?* I needed to escape sometimes. Unless I was at school or at Guides, I was stuck within the confines of the bungalow.

My parents organised a family holiday to Paignton for the three of us for a week, and Nicky went into kennels. It was the first time we'd been on holiday in four years. We tried to enjoy it, but we were like lost souls wandering around; we missed Nicky. I felt I had to be extra happy in order to help my parents feel pleased they had made the effort.

On our return, my father drove out to the dog kennels to pick up Nicky during a work lunch break, but came back with the wrong poodle. The kennels had realised their mistake and were chasing my father home with Nicky, hoping that the other poodle didn't run away before they arrived. My mother said immediately: 'You have the wrong dog!' My father looked confused as the van containing Nicky screeched around the corner into our road.

My mother had a pen friend from Australia, Mary, who she had written to since a child. Mary and her husband came over to stay. They loved walking and Nicky was in his element going out with them. When they left, Nicky was nowhere to be seen. We hunted for him. Then my father roamed about the village asking anyone if they'd seen him. Soon everyone was looking out for Nicky. I was sitting in the lounge, as usual, and kept hearing a noise I didn't recognise. Nicky had gone to mope in the wardrobe and my mother, not realising, had shut him in there. What a relief that he was safe!

When Nicky was seven, he got mauled by a farm dog while out on a lead in the countryside and never really recovered.

We bought another poodle who we called Judy. She was so sweet and gentle, and again she adored my father and jumped onto his lap as soon as he sat down. By then I was older and going out more. Judy pined if my parents went out. It was lovely having a dog but it didn't solve the problem. I still felt trapped.

One evening, when my parents were out for the evening, I was having a rummage in a cupboard and came across a shoe box. Intrigued, I had a look inside and saw old-style photo wallets containing bundles of photo negatives, but no photos. I held one up to the light. The photo showed young children playing with my father and an unknown woman. Could that be my real mother?

I had never seen a photo of my mother, so didn't know what she looked like. I spent most of the evening studying the photos trying to catch a glimpse of what my life had been like when I was young. I was fascinated. Here was a precious link to my past.

I wondered where the photos were, or even if they still existed. I had once asked my father if there were any photos of my birth mother, but he'd replied, quite abruptly, 'I don't want to upset your mother,' and walked away. Of course, he meant Kath.

I didn't mention finding the negatives to my parents, but I was so pleased that they'd not thrown away the negatives. I borrowed a few at a time and took the negatives in to have prints made when possible. I made my own secret photo album. I saw photos of my grandmother and cousins playing in the sand with Stuart and me. I treasured them.

I was fifty when my parents moved from their bungalow to a flat, and my mother gave me a photo album containing all the photos of my young life. I accepted it, but I never admitted that I'd already had a similar album for many years.

CHAPTER 32

I Challenge Myself

I immersed myself in Guiding, which I loved. My father pushed me to the Village Hall every Friday evening, having to haul me up three big steps in my wheelchair. I wanted to get my First Class Badge: to do this there was a long list of badges and activities I had to challenge myself with. I had only the more difficult challenges to achieve.

When Guides had finished one evening, many Guides collected their bikes just by the entrance to the hall to ride home, and they noticed that all the tyres had been slashed. The village policeman was informed in the hope that he could catch the culprit one evening. My father decided to take it upon himself to try and help. He hid in the bushes and waited. He was caught by the policeman, who immediately marched him into the hall. I had to admit that I knew him, this was my father! I can't *imagine* how embarrassed my father was that day. I'm sure he wasn't laughing.

I had to pass the Back Woman's badge, which included rigging-up a shelter and cooking a meal outdoors. Although it wasn't easy for me to do, I knew how to do this and the Guides in my patrol were keen to help me as I gave the instructions. It was arranged that a Guider would visit to assess the results. The day went well, we all pulled together and we were pleased with our achievements, but the Guider didn't turn up. She thought the challenge was impossible for me to achieve.

Another section of the First Class Badge was to walk six miles on a hike. I had never walked very far as I soon got tired and my callipers hurt me. I asked if there was an alternative and was told no, obviously to put me off.

At school, I was involved in the Duke of Edinburgh's Award, aiming for my Bronze Award. It required a six-mile hike. I thought that if I could walk the six miles, I'd pass both the First Class badge and the Duke of Edinburgh's Award.

I started to plan.

My parents thought I was crazy but were willing to help. They didn't think I'd get very far. Yvonne was helping at Guides at the time and agreed to come with me. We worked out a circular route along some country lanes. So, on Sunday, 15 March 1964, after Church Parade, we started walking towards Dipford. I found it easier to stand behind the wheelchair and push it as the wheelchair was more stable to hold onto. My walking was slow and I think Yvonne found it hard to keep at my pace.

It was a lovely day with blue skies and no wind, so we plodded on. I was determined to do this. We kept our minds occupied by observing the countryside. Progress was very slow as we wandered along the quiet country road. It took me an hour to walk one mile. It was the furthest I'd ever walked, and I just kept going. We sat down for a quick lunch and then walked on. My callipers and brace were beginning to rub, but I was determined to carry on.

The challenge looked daunting as the country road stretched ahead. We stopped at a house along the way in the hope of a downstairs toilet, and no, there wasn't one, but they did have a commode. By mid-afternoon we'd been on the road for five hours and I had walked four miles. My father arrived on his scooter to see how we were getting on. He said he'd put a large cross in the road at the six-mile point.

It didn't matter how tired I was or how stiff I was – I wasn't giving up. Yvonne and I chatted away as she slowly walked beside me. It was about 8.00 p.m. in the evening when one of us looked around and noticed a large cross in the road. We'd walked right over it without noticing. We'd done it.

I'd done it!

Both Yvonne and I were exhausted, but so excited. I'd been walking for eight hours. I felt as though we'd climbed Mount Everest. I had *shown* them. They'd have to give me the First Class Badge now and the Bronze Duke of Edinburgh's Award.

All was quiet for a while, but someone sent a report into the weekly newspaper. HTV television wanted to interview me. The interviewer met me at Brownies where I'd started to help. There was great excitement as the film crew arrived, and both Yvonne and I were interviewed. I attained my First Class Badge and my Bronze Award. In May, I attended a Guide service and received a Badge of Fortitude from the Guide Association. More people wanted to interview me.

In the summer, my parents received a letter. I'd been awarded the 'Bravest Girl of 1964'. I had also been awarded the 'Plus Ultra' award by the Spanish Government. I was invited to join a group of other brave children from around Europe for a holiday. The trip was sponsored by Iberian Airlines and the Spanish Television Company.

There was a rush to get ready. I had to wear a uniform, which was provided, to ensure we all looked the same. I wore a grey skirt, white blouse, navy blue jacket for travelling, but could wear green and white striped T-shirts for leisure. Even the suitcases were supplied so that we would all look the same.

The organisers specified black shoes. I had only a pair of brown shoes. I couldn't just go out and buy a pair of shoes, they had to be specially made to fit the callipers. My parents approached the hospital but the administrators there said I had received my allotted shoes for the year, so no more. Eventually the organisation agreed to pay the hospital in order to get a special pair of black shoes.

I was going abroad to Spain for a month with fifteen other children from around Europe. Iberian Airlines paid for a Spanish nurse to accompany me to Spain. It was like a dream come true.

I was *so* excited!

CHAPTER 33

Plus Ultra Award Holiday

I was the only disabled child in the group. We arrived in Madrid, staying in a hotel for a few days in order to meet each other. There were fifteen children between the ages of 5 years and 15 years. Each child had been brave in some way.

One girl from Germany, aged 10, had saved her brother when he fell into a gravel pit and was buried alive. She had moved the gravel with her hands. A girl from France had saved someone from a fire; the girl from Portugal had fought off a wolf with a stick when it attacked her brother; one lad had carried a disabled friend on his back to school every day; and the youngest child, aged five, helped to save her brother from the river.

We spent our first evening on the stage in front of a crowd of people wanting to know all about us. There were translators, journalists and photographers all trying to get a good story.

We left Spain and flew to Rome. The first hotel was not accessible for me, so my nurse Charo and I stayed at the Cavalier Hilton Hotel. We slept there for two days, revelling in the luxurious suite. We even had a basin each in the bathroom.

We were to have an audience with the Pope. He was in his summer residence at Castel del Gadolfo. We boarded the coach and drove through the countryside; the children started singing a Spanish song and Charo tried to teach me the words. The coach slowed down as we passed through a village. Lots of schoolchildren were lining the sides of the road, waving and cheering with flags and scarves. Word had spread and everyone wanted to meet us, and we waved back with lots of enthusiasm. I hadn't realised it would be like this. Everywhere we went, it was the same.

My first impression as we entered the building was that it resembled a large Cathedral with jewels all round, glittering as the light fell on them. There were tiers of seats along both sides and a long aisle down the centre. At the far end was a golden throne, with royal blue velvet curtains either side, where I was soon to see the Pope.

It was magnificent. The carpet was a rich dark velvety red, so thick that the wheels of my chair hardly moved, getting stuck. Pictures hung around the walls with golden cords hanging from them, sparkling in the light. There must've been over a thousand people seated.

There was a hush.

I stared, unblinking, as I saw the Pope in a golden chair fixed onto a platform, being carried to his throne. Four ornately-clothed soldiers carried the corners of the platform. The Pope was dressed all in white, and he waved to everyone as he made his way to the golden chair. He was lowered to the ground, and then sat on the throne. The platform was taken away.

When all was quiet, the Pope began to speak, in his rich and confident voice. This lasted for two hours. After each speech, the Pope waved and the great crowd cheered and clapped. I couldn't understand anything he said, but looked around at the splendour of it all.

Charo whispered 'Now is the time to meet the Pope'. Six of us were chosen, including me, and we waited behind the royal blue curtains. We walked down the aisle, with Charo pushing me, in single file, and stood in front of the Pope. I didn't know what I should do. I tried to see what other people were doing.

They were kissing his hand. It was actually his ring they were kissing, but I didn't know that then. My turn came. The Pope held out his hand to me. I was trembling as I took his hand to kiss it. The Pope said 'Where are you from?' and I replied 'England.' He said 'I will bless your country, your family, and you.' I said 'Thank you' and I was pushed away in my wheelchair. Something was pressed into my hand. In the coach, I discovered it was a small gold coin, the size of a florin, in a protective cover. One side was engraved with the head and shoulders of Pope Paul, and the reverse bore a Coat of Arms.

We visited both the English and Italian Embassies, where we were given tea and presents. We visited a children's home and we exchanged presents, playing games with the children before leaving. On the way back to the hotel we had a sightseeing tour of Rome.

Next stop was Barcelona, but we ran into a storm and had to land in Majorca for the night. As we stepped out of the plane, crowds of people cheered and a band played. Little children ran up to us, giving us each a bunch of flowers and a present. They made a circle around us on the tarmac and danced. We waved to everyone as we boarded the coach and climbed a steep road to the hotel.

We spent the morning in a funfair. It felt good just to play for a while. We tried various rides for free. In the afternoon, we had a cable car ride high across Barcelona. The cable car moved in the wind as I tried to walk across the gap from the pylon to the cable car. I froze, I thought: *I might do the splits!* It was worrying. But someone grabbed me and lifted me on. There was no room for my wheelchair. We all stood looking down at Barcelona below us as we travelled across the city.

We travelled by plane onwards to Majorca the same day.

The next day we set off for a cave called the Cavern of the Dragon. Ten men lifted me down the many steps to the bottom. The steps were wet and slippery with nothing to hang onto. My wheelchair and I lunged from one position to the other as I tried to grip. Parts of the cave were lit and many of the huge stalactites and stalagmites reached the floor of the cave and up to the roof. When we reached the bottom of the cave there was a lovely emerald green shimmering lake. Illuminated boats slowly swirled into view. They were filled with musicians and their instruments, and everyone sat quietly to listen to the classical music floating across the lake. The acoustics were amazing. It was very emotional and awe-inspiring. After the show, rowing boats came to take us over to the other side of the lake.

Once again, the men arrived to lift me into the boat and, manually, out the other side. Then I heard there were 80 steps to get out of the cave. Perspiration rolled off them as the men struggled to lift me up the rock-carved steps. All I could do was sit still and hope that no-one would slip or fall. It was a truly hair-raising experience.

We spent the afternoon on the beach and in the sea. A few of the children had never been to the coast before. We all had the same swimwear. The heat of the sun was really fierce and the only shade on the beach was to be found with straw sunshades pushed into the ground. The sand was soft, silky and warm, and by the edge of the road, tufts of grass grew. I sat by the edge of the sea and let the small waves rush past me.

I got very sunburnt that day. It hurt if anyone just touched my shoulders. Charo ordered a jug of warm water, mixed with vinegar, for the bath. It helped a little, but for some days afterwards I flinched if I thought anyone was going to touch my shoulders.

The following day we went to a bullfight. The bull was going to be teased, but not killed. The ring was quite small and covered in sand. We watched a demonstration and then they asked for volunteers. They asked if anyone from our party would like to try. The oldest boy, who was Spanish, came forward. We cheered when he returned, very obviously pleased with himself.

Rising early the next day, we flew to Madrid and then onwards to Malaga. Once again we were met by children, who gave us flowers, sweets and raisins. They entertained us by dancing some typical dances of the south of Spain, Andalucia. They wore bright dresses, with carnations in their hair. Again, our hotel was by the sea. Later, we went to sleep with the sound of the waves crashing against the rocks beneath our windows.

We went to see another bullfight, where the bull was teased. One of the boys in our group became the $1,000^{th}$ visitor and he was presented with a large toy bull, a felt hat and a banner to put across his shoulders. He had to enter the ring, opening the gate for the bull. We cheered him when he returned to his seat. We had supper at the hotel that evening. It was too hot to sleep, so Charo and I dressed in our swimming costumes and had an evening dip in the pool. It was a lovely experience for just the two of us to be together and enjoy the cool water.

The following day, we flew on to Santiago, via Madrid. On our arrival children gave us bunches of flowers. Our hotel formed part of a large square courtyard called the Obradoiro Square. We stayed in a famous hotel that had been both a palace and a wartime hospital in the past. Around the square was the famous and magnificent Santiago de Compostela Catholic Church, which is on a pilgrim route. News of our visit spread and crowds began to gather. We walked across the square to visit the Bishop of Santiago. We each kissed his hand and he blessed us. We then walked across the courtyard again to visit the Government building to be introduced to the Mayor. There were crowds of people waiting outside to see us. The Mayor allowed us to stand on a balcony to wave to them. I couldn't believe that so many people wanted to see us.

In the evening, we watched more Spanish dancing in the square. This took place on a high platform for everyone to enjoy, and the square was packed with people. We were getting squashed as people tried to meet us; so we were lifted onto the stage with the dancers, and everyone cheered. The dancers wore bright costumes and danced to loud Flamenco music for the whole evening. The atmosphere was electric.

We attended a service in the huge Cathedral. There was a massive swinging incense burner, with a lot of men pulling on a single rope to hoist the incense burner and make it sway back and forth along the main aisle. It was at least four feet of heavy metal. It was an impressive sight, and the incense filled our lungs.

We also had an audience with General Franco at his summer residence. I wasn't sure of his importance, but followed everyone into a small room to chat with photographers. It was an ordinary room with a few old fashioned armchairs, and a beautiful old polished wooden table with round clawed feet.

We met General Franco in his office. He was dressed in a plain dark suit. He pinned a medal to my blazer which said La Merito Civil. He then handed out the medals laid in a royal blue velvet and satin box to the other children.

We were ushered into the garden and given ice-cream and Coca Cola. We had a group photo taken with General Franco and were then escorted back to the coach. The whole visit had only lasted an hour. I couldn't stop looking at my medal. It was so unexpected.

While in Santiago, we visited a boys home, a Coca Cola factory, a football team, a radio station and a naval base. In the evenings, we had meals with various mayors. By that time, many of us were so tired all we wanted to do was sleep.

I was surprised by a gentleman who gave me a photo of himself. He had artificial legs and hoped it would encourage me to keep trying. People gave us presents wherever we went.

We flew on to Tenerife and were again entertained by children dancing, and our hotel was once again by the sea. We saw rows of banana plantations along the way and we were offered quite a few to eat. We boarded a coach to visit the volcano, Mount Teide. We had to drive up through narrow twisty roads. We drove through mist, giving way to brilliant sunshine. When we looked down, all we could see was the mist creeping up the hillside as though there was nothing below us. Around the next corner we saw Mount Teide and kept driving towards the top of the volcano.

We wandered around. There was lava everywhere, glistening in the sun. I picked some up and as I flashed the black lava rock, there were several different colours caught in the brightness. We spent quite a few hours there and then visited a hotel nearby for a meal.

The following morning we spent time looking around the Botanical Gardens. Cacti grew as tall as trees, there were gum trees with trunks as thick as a car, and monkeys swung between the trees.

Then we flew to Las Palmas. We had a tour of the island and stopped at a beach for a swim. We visited a small town, where one of the girls in our party lived. She helped her sisters there, who were disabled. There were banners across the street. Everyone cheered as we arrived and they offered us refreshments.

Las Palmas Cathedral was the next location on our agenda, and we saw the highly-decorated statute of The Madonna and Child. There were emeralds and diamonds set in necklaces around her neck and a large ruby was set in a band around her forehead. Once outside, we enjoyed a carnival.

There was so much happening.

The trip ended. We'd been together for nearly a month and had formed a real bond, despite the language differences. We were sad to say goodbye. We hugged one another, knowing that we would probably never see each other again. As I went towards my plane, a group of Girl Guides were waiting to see me with their leader. They presented me with a large felt doll, about 2 foot long, made and dressed by them. They pinned the Spanish friendship badge onto me.

On our return, we visited the Guide Headquarters in Buckingham Palace Road, where a TV presenter interviewed me about the trip. Then Charo, my nurse accompanied me home. We had enjoyed so much fun together, how could I say goodbye? We were met by our parents and the Divisional Commissioner of Taunton, all happy to know I was safe and well.

I had been so happy and I'd never forget the people we met, the gifts we received, the places we visited. The Spanish trip had offered me a wealth of new, wonderful experiences and another opportunity for independence. I realised what I could achieve in the future, and hung onto that thought. It was as though a new world had been opened up for me.

CHAPTER 34

A Waiting Game

In September, I started my two-year GCE exam course. I chose six subjects, but I didn't include Maths – not my best subject. This was my last year at Askwith Secondary School. The following year I was due to start at Castle School, a brand-new school.

In the spring, my mother needed a hysterectomy. The consultant agreed that I could stay in hospital until my mother had recovered. I wasn't sure why this was thought necessary, as I was now mostly independent, but the decision had been made.

I entered the hospital yet again for an unknown time. I was so pleased to see Pauline there. I often wondered why she'd spent her entire life in hospital. In a way, she'd been my best friend throughout my early years. We never stayed in touch when I left hospital and yet we were happy to continue our friendship whenever we met. I wasn't to know this would be our last time together: Pauline died later that year. I will always remember her. She helped me so much.

I remember during this stay in hospital that Pauline and I (both Girl Guides) were given the opportunity to visit a Jamboree in Bath, where Lady Baden-Powell, who had started the Girl Guides, was giving a speech. We sat near the platform as Lady Baden-Powell approached. As she put her hand up, all those hundreds of people became quiet. It was an amazing experience.

It was around that time that the consultant decided I'd finished growing, and could wear an ordinary back support brace; so the neckpiece was removed. For the first time in five years, I was able to look down and around. *That* was a relief. It may have stopped my curvature getting any worse, but it hadn't improved it. I could also dispense with the plaster bed and metal boots at night.

I could sleep, now, exactly how I wanted – what a luxury!

There was a negative side to wearing the brace. I had worn a spinal support for so long, I found it even harder to sit up without a brace. Within half an hour I had awful backache. My stomach muscles had become flabby, as they hadn't needed to work. Also, the muscles under my chin were sagging from not having to function. I was very conscious of that.

Time passed slowly in hospital because, this time, I didn't need treatment. Even the Occupational Therapy Department had changed. Gone were the days when I could pop down to make something. The emphasis was on getting people home now. The hospital social worker asked me if I would like to go away for a while; there was a week's course at a place called Avon Tyrell in the New Forest, which catered for disabled people. I agreed to go.

I packed what I had in hospital, an extra dress, cardigan, nightwear and toiletries. Ambulance men picked me up early on Saturday morning and by 10.00

a.m. I arrived with my small bag on the front doorstep of a large building. The organisers said I was too early, and so I was shown into the library.

I stayed in the library all day. There was no offer of lunch or a drink. I grew more and more nervous. *Maybe I'd a made a mistake in agreeing to come.* As I looked out of the window, I watched people starting to arrive. I couldn't see any children, only adults, and they all knew one another.

Later on the door suddenly opened and a lady asked if I would like some dinner. I followed her to the dining room where other people were eating. I sat quietly eating, letting the conversation carry on around me. I always felt awkward with adults and hadn't done a lot of socialising. At fifteen, I was the only child there.

Everyone went to the bar and sat around talking. Someone asked me what I would like to drink and I shook my head. I had never been anywhere with a bar before so didn't know what to drink, and also I had no money. I asked where the toilets were and they pointed outside. I tried to hold back my tears as I realised the week was going to be very different to what I'd expected. Then I disappeared back to the library. I didn't read, I just hid until it was time to go to bed. The bedrooms were upstairs with no lifts; anyone not able to climb up the stairs was carried in their wheelchair, and that included me.

The next day we could choose various activities. Some courses needed a contribution. Because of my money situation, I looked for the free activities. There was swimming, but I had no swimming costume. I decided on archery and woodwork. I enjoyed archery and the woodwork tutor helped me make a small wooden tray in the shape of a leaf. Every evening I escaped to the library. I wanted to be part of the group but no-one helped me. I think they assumed I was an adult who wanted to read.

On Thursday morning, I felt hot and feverish. The nurse said I had a temperature and was advised to stay in bed. I stayed there until I left on the Saturday. I had no money to buy the small tray I'd made but, as I was leaving, the woodwork tutor ran out and gave it to me.

I was so glad to be back in hospital again, but had to stay in the side ward until I was better.

Once on the ward, I met a new girl, Suzanna – she was in the next bed. We soon became friends and gave each other nicknames. I called her Squashed Grape as she was always losing them in her bed. Suzanna called me Gone off Banana because I usually left any bananas. Her parents brought in the drink Tizer for her, and I tried some and loved it. My parents said 'No' to Tizer, but I asked for some money and gave it to Suzanna. Her parents bought some for me. One day Suzanna's parents brought us both water pistols. We had so much fun trying to squirt each other without warning. Eventually, we were caught and the pistols were taken away. No doubt my father would get another lecture.

Meanwhile, my mother was recuperating in Torquay. Suzanna and I wrote to each other for ages using these nicknames when we left hospital.

I returned home in June. I'd spent the whole of the summer term in hospital. This had been the first year of my GCE exams; I'd taken schoolbooks into hospital but it was so hard to concentrate and learn without any tuition, and with the constant distraction. It was nearly the end of term and our time at this school. The Beatles had just released a song called

Yesterday. It seemed an appropriate song as we remembered the happy times at the school we were leaving behind.

I was told that a few weeks away had been organised for me, to help my mother's continuing recuperation. One of the weeks was a Red Cross holiday in Bristol with other disabled children around my age. Some young Red Cross cadets came to help. The older Red Cross nurses fussed after us as we tried different activities. One of the cadets bought a sexy novel in a nearby charity shop. It was all about seduction and romance. The book was so popular, we took it in turns to read a chapter. When it was my turn, I disappeared into the dorm and became absorbed. Suddenly the door opened and an older Red Cross nurse approached me. Looking highly embarrassed, I stuffed the book down the side of my wheelchair and tried to sit on it. 'What were you reading?' she asked. I just stared at her. There was no way I was going to hand over the book. She said she'd heard we were reading Black Beauty, and then she walked away. I sighed with relief.

I'd been chosen to represent England at a Guide Camp in Germany for disabled girls. Mary, a Ranger who was going to help me, travelled with me to Germany. We stayed with a family in Mainz for a week and then we travelled to the campsite in Darmstadt. The disabled campers slept inside a hostel, but I asked to sleep in a tent with Mary. We explored the area and had fun trying to communicate with the other girls.

In the evenings, we had to pass by the tethered guard dog and run towards our tent before lights out. I was crawling into bed when I came nose to nose with the guard dog who'd been let loose. We froze as he growled and sniffed around me. I kept very still until he wandered away, and then I could breathe easy again.

We had trips out to explore the area, on one occasion going on a pleasure boat for a trip along the Rhine. I remember visiting a cathedral with the group and a few of us couldn't get up the steps, so we waited patiently outside. Someone came over and gave us each some money, and then walked away. Did they think we were begging? I couldn't speak German to explain, so decided to go and buy an ice cream.

CHAPTER 35

CHURCHYARD TRIP

My father had just passed his driving test, and one weekend some relatives stayed with us and, as they were leaving, my father offered to go ahead in his car to help them get onto the right road. He asked if I would like to accompany him, so I seized the chance, and I did.

As we waved them off, my father turned to me and asked if I'd like to see where my mother was buried. This came as a total surprise as I'd never been able to get my father to talk about my birth mother. I had no idea where my mother had been buried.

We weren't far away, my mother was buried in the grounds of the Baptist Church in North Curry, a small village, in the middle of nowhere near the Somerset levels. As we parked the car, I noticed there were steep steps up to the churchyard. My father helped to pull me up the steps and I followed him to a flat piece of the church's grounds, where he pointed. It looked rather sad. There was no gravestone to say who'd been buried there, just a rather worn metal vase placed there by the neighbours.

Everyone else had gravestones.

My memory of her was lost, as was any mention of her in the churchyard. I looked at the countryside around, it was so peaceful there. I was glad that she'd been buried in such a lovely place. While I was struggling to get down the steps, I fell and landed in a heap on the road. My father helped me up and into the car. He then surprised me again by showing me the outside of the cottage where my mother grew up with her sisters.

As my father drove home, my right leg pounded with pain; I'd sprained my ankle in the fall. I told my father. He was horrified and said there was no way I could tell my mother where I'd been. When we arrived home, I climbed out of the car and the pain shot up my leg as I limped into the kitchen. My mother immediately pounced on me, and asked why was I limping? I said that I'd fallen as I'd got out of the car. My mother replied that there was no need to get out of the car, was there, I was only waving someone off.

I kept quiet.

It was all so difficult. I wanted to tell her where I'd been but knew then my father would be in trouble. Why did there have to be this kind of charade, everyone treading carefully around each other! I received no sympathy as I hobbled around in my callipers until the pain subsided. The good side of things was that I'd gained some small information about my birth mother. I now knew where she'd lived. I drove to the village again and wandered around, trying to imagine how she had lived back in the day, and I took in the small school building she'd attended, which was no longer a school. Things had changed.

Following that, I couldn't visit my mother's grave for a long time, but I drove past a few years ago and could see that there is now a ramp to the churchyard, so I could visit.

After my parents' death in recent years, I sought permission to put a flat stone on my birth mother's grave site. I owed it to her, and even though I remembered nothing much of her, she was my real mother and had loved me.

Now she was *no longer* invisible. At last, her life and death had been properly marked – by me, all those years later.

CHAPTER 36

New School

In 1966, I entered my new – newly-built – school in my wheelchair, and found it to be totally inaccessible. All the classrooms were upstairs, and there was no lift. There were steps into the hall. This was still the time when all disabled children went away to a special school, so there was no need for a school to be wheelchair accessible.

I was in my final year at school and would be taking my 'GCE' exams the following June. It was an important year for me. To begin with, the staff and older pupils lifted me in my manual wheelchair up and down the stairs, but came to realise they couldn't cope with it. A table was put in the school corridor, and that became my desk for the year.

I hated it. I missed the interaction and atmosphere of working with my classmates. What were they being taught, which I wasn't part of? Usually, someone came down to give me school work, and sometimes they forgot. I stared at the blank walls and found it hard to concentrate. Schoolwork had been a big challenge with all those months in hospital, and I was always behind the other students. As the months dragged on, I became disillusioned, and basically stopped bothering. No-one checked to see if I was okay.

I took my mock exams and failed all of them. Of course, my parents gave me a lecture. I wasn't going to get a job unless I had some qualifications. So I decided to have another go at studying; every evening I sat in my wheelchair in my bedroom, studying. I had six months to catch up.

Then, just to add to my school problems, the consultant wanted me have my first ever operation. My ankle was bending outwards, making it difficult for me to walk. This included six weeks in plaster afterwards. I couldn't believe the timing for the last few months I had to study. I read and re-read The Merchant of Venice, The Inspector Calls and other school books.

The operation hadn't worked.

I passed 5 GCEs but not English Language. The grades were low, but they were a pass. I was so surprised – along with everyone else.

The school then organised different sports activities. I chose archery. I had to admit that I couldn't see the target very well. The tutor suggested that I visit an optician. The optician discovered that I was indeed quite short-sighted and asked how I'd managed without glasses for so long. The school optician had always blamed my poor vision on my brace.

Everything looked so clear with glasses on. Was this how other people saw the world? I couldn't stop looking around in amazement! I could read signs at a distance. The television screen looked so crisp and clear. What a difference it would've made if I'd grown up wearing glasses. My parents had no idea.

I was now 16 and the government issued me with what they called an Invalid Carriage. They were three-wheeled trikes based on motorbike technology with a tiller bar, and made of fibre glass. They were all painted blue, and known by disabled people as Noddy Cars. There was just the driver's seat and a space at the side for a wheelchair. I saw this as my chance for freedom and couldn't wait. I didn't need a driving test, just a provisional driving licence. Everyone else driving on the roads needed a driving licence except for disabled people!

The allocated driving instructor arrived for the first of my three driving lessons. After that, I was on my own. I had to follow him in his own car as there was only the driver's seat. I didn't even know how to change gear. We set off. I followed the driving instructor out of our road and turned right onto the main road. I turned right too quickly and slid off the seat, landing on the floor of the car. As I was still hanging onto the accelerator stick, my car continued driverless. Shaken but determined not to get lost, I managed to get back onto the seat, and continued.

My father had just passed his driving test, and I followed him gaining confidence, slowly. One day I drove under the arm of a policeman as he was whistling for me to stop. I was so busy concentrating, I didn't see him. He wasn't impressed but I was allowed to continue.

One of the first things I did, once I was proficient with my trike, was to drive to a hairdressers for my very first professional haircut. It was a great feeling to be so in control of what I wanted to do – at last.

My parents had complained to the Education Authority about the poor facilities at the new school. The Education

Department agreed that I could board at Florence Treloar School for disabled girls in Hampshire for two years in the sixth form.

I was very surprised. I'd often wondered what life might've been like if I'd gone away to school. Now I was going to find out. *What if I didn't fit in!* I was nervous, but excited at the same time, of course.

CHAPTER 37

FLORENCE TRELOAR SCHOOL

My parents drove through the gates of my new school and helped me unload my luggage. All around us other girls were doing the same, most of whom knew each other.

This was suddenly beginning to feel very real.

I was to share a room with two other girls in the blue corridor of the accommodation block. It seemed strange saying goodbye to my parents this time. I'd said this to them so many times in the past without really thinking. Hospital had been like a second home to me; now I'd come to a completely different environment where I knew no-one, and was even further from home.

It's always difficult to fit in with a group of girls who knew the routine and already had friends. It was good to be with a group of girls rather than be on my own, but I was shy with people I didn't know. I wanted to fit in, but knew it would take time. There were other girls my age, and slightly older in the sixth form, all trying to improve their education.

This was a pioneering school for disabled girls. My education had been so basic, and this was my chance to really learn. The thinking at that time, generally, was that disabled children weren't expected to get jobs and be independent, but to be cared for all their lives. I didn't want that, and neither did my parents wish that for me.

Florence Treloar School, which opened its doors two years previously, was one of the first schools to expect disabled girls to be educated at the same level as other pupils and achieve equality in adult live. Some of the girls gained places in university, which was virtually unheard of in the 1960s. Florence Treloar School wanted to change perceptions of disabled people. There was also a Lord Mayor Treloar College for boys.

But I was soon to find that the rules were strict, and punctuality important. The deputy head teacher watched us file in for meal times, especially at breakfast, and was ready to apprehend anyone who was late. It always seemed to take longer for me, having to put on my brace and callipers, and there were times when I only just made it. The tables at mealtimes held eight people. There was someone from each age group plus a tutor. This changed each week, and we rushed to the notice board to see who we would be sitting with, and with which tutor. At some point we would be with the Headmistress or Deputy Headmistress, which was daunting for me. It was quite overwhelming at times, but a way of getting to know people.

We had our own sixth form common room with a small kitchen at the side where we could relax; not that I found time to relax much once the school routine was under way.

I was at the school for two years; just right to study some 'A' levels. There was a problem though, there was no-one else ready to take 'A' levels, so they were not part of the curriculum for this year. I was disappointed. I was there for two years, so I needed to do something. I agreed to take English Language, Human Biology, History and Music. I'd wanted to give up piano lessons and music in general, but the music teacher was eager for me to continue, and it was another exam to have to take. My lack of Maths knowledge meant that I didn't have to attend the lessons because I didn't have the necessary background.

Every morning we filed into the main hall for assembly of hymns and prayers. I could feel the eyes of the teachers scrutinising us, our uniform, how we sat and how we sang. One morning I heard my name announced: I was not singing properly. I had to report to the choir master and join the choir. But he soon let me go. That was a relief to me.

We often congregated in the hall for talks from outside speakers. Everyone was told to report to the hall for the talks, and it always amused me when the speaker said how nice it was to see so many of us.

I found the talks interesting.

I remember Gerald Durrell, who established a zoo in Jersey, coming to give a talk. Also someone from a Russian Orthodox Church gave a talk, and I was part of the group who visited the Russian Orthodox Cathedral in London, which I found fascinating.

On Saturday mornings, the sixth form students had to be in charge of the classrooms while the younger pupils did their homework. I found this quite intimidating. The younger pupils wanted to impress, but the older pupils tried to challenge our authority. I realised what it'd been like for my teachers when we'd played-up at school.

Whatever the weather, every Sunday morning we dressed in uniform and walked to the local church. We were directed to the side pews. We had to be at church before the congregation entered, and be the last to leave. Sunday afternoons were free but there was a film showing in the hall and we were all expected to attend. The films were mostly quite old, but I did enjoy them. In a way, it was like being at a mini cinema, minus the ice creams of course.

The school uniform was apple green blouses and grey skirts with dark green jumpers. I'd never really been aware of what other girls wore; my homemade dresses looked very basic compared to the girls at Florence Treloar. I decided to wear my school uniform most of the time, making excuses of not having enough time to change.

I needed to get some nicer clothes.

There was a large swimming pool on site. I was automatically enrolled for the swimming club, canoe club and the water volleyball club. I didn't excel in any of them. I couldn't understand how I was meant to throw a ball in water and not go under, as my legs didn't work to keep me afloat. I often heard my name called out. Eventually, I was only part of the team if they were desperate. That suited me very well.

The canoe club was the worst. With a weak back, I found it hard to keep the canoe steady. I had to learn how to roll over, come out of the canoe, and reach the surface. In my first attempt, I rolled over, but my foot got stuck. I was under the water, desperate to get out. I panicked and started to swim. The canoe hit the side of the swimming pool, which dislodged my foot and I gasped for air as I surfaced.

I had a lecture on how not to damage expensive canoes. I felt I couldn't win.

The Guide Leader asked if I could assist her with the school Guide Company, and of course I agreed. She wanted me to plan an evening. When I turned up on my first evening, I was told that the Guide Leader couldn't attend. I was on my own with the Guides, so I put my plan into action. I realised that some of my games needed to be adapted, but completed the meeting. The Guide Leader, also the Deputy Headmistress, wanted to see how I coped. After the first scary session, I did enjoy helping the Guides. The Deputy Headmistress took me with her to a couple of Guiders events and we organised a Guide Camp near Poole.

In the needlework classes, the sewing machines were manual, so I could use them. I gradually started making a few things. The History teacher brought her golden retriever into class, who followed her everywhere; we all welcomed a visiting dog. The piano teacher gave me individual piano lessons, but I mostly worked on my own. The tutor in cookery classes always challenged me, as I had an 'O' level in Home Economics.

There was a first floor above our accommodation block, which was the staff accommodation. The Headmistress held weekly discussion groups for the sixth form students in the upstairs lounge. We went up by lift to discuss various topics and I was happy to listen to girls chatting away, putting forward their opinions.

On one occasion, the Headmistress suddenly looked at me and asked for my opinion. *Me?* Why would I have an opinion? My mother had always seen any opinion as a threat to her authority; I'd stopped trying to have opinions long ago. The girls turned to me as I looked back at her in horror. I couldn't speak, and the silence lengthened. The Headmistress saw this as insubordination, a black mark. *How could I explain?* It was years before I was to have the confidence to express any views.

At half-term, my parents took me to stay with some friends in Winchester. I asked if I could have some different clothes. It was still difficult to find clothes to fit over my brace and callipers, but I bought two very flared bright orange and cerise felt- type skirts. Unfortunately, I forgot to buy some tops to go with them. I had only dresses at school. So, again, I carried on wearing my school uniform.

I was gradually getting to know the girls. I was involved in a midnight feast, which seemed such an exciting thing to do. One of the girls bought a chicken along with some snacks and we put the chicken in the oven to cook for later. I sneaked out with a few girls in the dark to retrieve the chicken from the sixth form oven. We all squeezed into one room to eat, keeping as quiet as possible.

I brought some local cider from home for our next feast. As Jane couldn't sit up in bed, we gave her a straw to use. The next day, Jane giggled non-stop. Apparently, cider is more potent if drunk through a straw. I didn't know that, and neither did anyone else at the time.

The upstairs lounge had a television. On a few occasions we were allowed to watch a late night film on a Saturday night. They were mainly horror and crime films. I wasn't keen on the films, but loved being with the other girls sitting in a tight group, trying not to be scared, and then creeping back to bed afterwards in the dark.

The school organised events around the neighbouring area. We went to the local theatre to see plays, we visited local schools and in turn they were invited back. At half-term we went to the cinema and ten pin bowling. We'd never been far as a family and I revelled in these outings. I rarely went home at half-term, it was too far for a long weekend, and I would've spent most of my time travelling. I didn't mind.

Some of the girls had their Ministry three-wheeled vehicles at school. Mine was at home, so I asked if it could be transported to the school. It was agreed, but it was damaged in transit, so I had to wait months for a replacement. By the time it arrived, it was almost time for the summer holidays. I would be at home and my trike was at school. I didn't have the confidence to drive home, it was a long way to travel.

My mother sent me regular newsy letters about life at home. My dad usually added a note at the end, although sometimes he wrote his own letter. He hated writing. I enjoyed receiving post and I tried to write home as often as I could. Some girls phoned home, but I couldn't because my parents had no phone.

My mother sent me parcels, never food or sweets, but things she thought I'd like. She knitted me some brightly coloured, striped bed socks. I really liked them. I showed them to my friends and then had to ask my mother if she could knit some for other girls.

My mother and I got on much better at a distance. Even when I went home from school for holidays, we got on fairly well together for the short time I was there. It was as though she wanted to make up for me being away.

The school had its own consultant and every term we paraded in our underwear in front of him with the matron attending. We were prodded and poked. I still saw the consultant in Bath; my ankle was still causing a problem and he wanted to try another operation. I spent the Easter holidays in hospital and went back to school with my leg in plaster. Unfortunately, that operation didn't work either.

I passed my English Language, History and Music 'O' Level and had top marks for my Human Biology 'O' Level.

During the school holidays, my mother took me to a dressmaker for some new clothes. I had very high hopes for something pretty that actually fitted me.

CHAPTER 38

LORD MAYOR OF LONDON

The Treloar Trust had been named after the Lord Mayor of London. In 1908, Sir William Purdie Treloar established The Lord Mayor Treloar Hospital and College in Alton, Hampshire. Subsequent Lord Mayors of London had continued the interest and visited the school each year. Occasionally we had the opportunity to visit the Lord Mayor in his Mansion House in London.

About thirty of us were invited to the Mansion House in London for afternoon tea. Smartly dressed in uniform, we travelled to London. We visited a restaurant first for a meal, and sat at long tables in a separate room. The school nurse sat next to me at the end of the table and put her first-aid case down on the floor beside her. A waitress approached our table with a tray of glasses of tomato juice... and she fell right over the first-aid case. I watched as the glasses of tomato juice flew off the tray, catapulting the thick red juice over us all. We took our jackets off and the staff rushed away to clean them, and we were cleaned-up. Our Headmistress scrutinised us, determined to establish whether any of us had been at fault.

Looking respectable again, we drove to the Mansion House and were invited to sit around a very large long table. Smartly dressed waiters offered us dainty sandwiches and cups of tea. A lift took us down to the basement and we were shown the magnificent gold and silver collection for ceremonial use. A rare glimpse of history.

The sixth form were invited to a piano recital in aid of our school. The Mansion House looked regal as we sat at one end of the hall in our uniforms. Guests arrived in their evening gowns to take their seats. Some guests came over to speak with us about the school. We hadn't yet eaten, we knew there was food coming later on. The waiters offered us each a glass of wine, not something we were used to. The waiters offered us another glass of wine and we said 'Yes, please.'

As we started to giggle, our Headmistress realised she had a group of tipsy school children on show. She quickly ordered rolls for us to eat and glared at us, warning us not to misbehave.

Then we were each handed a plate of Chicken Supreme. After eating, we thanked the Mayor, and left, heading for the coach. As I stood up, an ornate fork clattered to the floor. I looked down in horror. I then remembered that we had been offered a fork, but the plate of food already had a fork, so I'd forgotten about the one on my lap.

I had to report to the Headmistress's office to convince her I hadn't intended to steal cutlery. Why was it always me!

The Lord Mayor of London visited our school to be shown around and to talk to us. The chauffeur waited by the Rolls Royce. We bravely asked if it was possible to go for a ride. He agreed and we formed a queue as he took us in small groups for a quick ride in his beautiful vehicle.

Beside the Lord Mayor of London coming to see us, there were other grand people. There was an elderly lady, who lived in a grand house close by the school who, I was told, was on good terms with the Queen Mother. Every term the lady sent an invitation to the school for two pupils to have tea with her. One term I was invited to go along with Judith.

The chauffeur drove us to her imposing house. We were shown into the lounge for a chat and a game of cards. We then sat at a huge table topped with all kinds of sandwiches and cakes. The waiter brought in a plate of warm crumpets oozing with butter. This lady was just happy to watch us eat; I wondered if she thought we didn't eat at school. There was so much food left when we'd finished; I hoped it wasn't going to be wasted. I shyly mentioned how the other girls would enjoy some food, and so we returned with boxes of food to hand around. Judith and I were *extremely* popular that day.

CHAPTER 39

YEAR TWO

This year, my second year at Florence Treloar, there were enough pupils to provide 'A' level classes in Geography and History. These were two-year courses and I only had one year left at the school. I was unlikely to finish the course, so felt this was all a waste of time, but began the course anyway.

I shared a bedroom with three other girls. Eileen had just started her first term, and I was to be her buddy. We got on well.

My Ministry three-wheeler was here. I drove around the country lanes and the local town of Holybourne to improve my driving skills. Eileen had her own three-wheeled vehicle but lacked confidence. One Sunday, a friend called Linda, Eileen and I drove around the lanes in our cars, with Eileen driving in the middle. All went well until we drove down a hill to a T-junction. Eileen went down the hill too fast and continued to cross the road and up the hedge the other side. We found Eileen shaken but unhurt; although her car was damaged. Fibreglass trikes split so easily.

A passing couple gave Eileen a lift back to school. Linda went to a garage for help and I stood guard by the car until it was towed away. I thought I might get into trouble again, but luckily I was only asked why I had missed the film back at school.

The English teacher suggested we attend a piano recital at a nearby college one evening. I asked if I could drive behind the bus in my vehicle to get used to the dark. I was fine following the minibus along the country lanes, but the driver was going too fast for me, and he disappeared. *Help!* I didn't know where I was meant to be going, I was relying on the minibus to lead me there. I didn't know how to get back to the school either.

I was lost.

I wandered around the country lanes in the dark looking for any sign that might help me. The school bus was also wandering around the lanes looking for me. Hooray, eventually we found one another, but we'd missed most of the recital.

My driving was improving and when I returned to school from a trip out, I did an efficient U-turn to park it. One of the girls was impressed and tried to do the same. Having not quite got the hang of it, she drove onto the grass and over the rose bushes. I disappeared quickly before I could get the blame.

We were putting on a Christmas play for parents at the end of term. My role was an angel. I had to stand on a box so that everyone could see me. I was not very good at standing for any length of time, and soon wobbled. It took all my strength to stay there, hanging onto something. I couldn't concentrate on the play, only on how not to fall off. Instead of seeing the angelic face of a nativity angel, they saw a terrified angel trying not to fall on everyone.

There was going to be a party afterwards in the common room. I said goodbye to my parents, who were staying overnight locally, and rushed off to my room with the other girls to get ready for the party. One of the girls had gone to bed early and I greeted her mother who was seated by her bed.

The next morning I was approached by the school administrator who asked me for Katherine's railway ticket. She said she had come to the bedroom the evening before to give Katherine her railway ticket, and as I was the only one around, she'd given me the train ticket for Katherine. I couldn't understand, as I hadn't been on my own at any time the evening before. I wondered if the administrator had forgotten to get the railway ticket and decided to blame me. The other girls had already left for home so I had no back-up. I explained the problem to my parents when they arrived; they believed me, but we searched the area and the bins just in case. I didn't think the Headmistress would believe me. When I returned to school, the administrator said she'd found the ticket in my wastepaper bin, which was clearly untrue. She'd never liked me. I'm not sure why.

I now had a room to myself. It was so good to have some privacy, and there was a desk for homework.

Three of us were doing 'A' Level Geography. The tutor, who was also the Deputy Headmistress, suggested we visit the Yorkshire Dales over Easter to explore the geographical features. She had her own caravan, and we rented one for the three of us. It was my first experience in a caravan. Getting in was a challenge as the caravan was not adapted in any way, and the steps going in were really steep. We had plenty of food. We had worked out a list of food to share and we'd all arrived with double the amount.

The tutor drove us everywhere, explaining the geographical features. There was so much to see. We walked beside meandering rivers, over limestone pavements and along scars. We had a terrific time together. One day we drove to the Lake District and marvelled at the views. We got back to our car one day to find that someone had broken in. All they had pinched was a homemade fruit cake.

At school, I was still working on my Duke of Edinburgh's Award. As part of this, I was required to organise a weekend away. Yvonne and Linda agreed to come with me, and I planned to visit the New Forest and stay in a youth hostel in Winchester. We studied the route thoroughly.

We each set off to drive in our Ministry three-wheelers to the New Forest. We drove in a convoy, keeping close together. All was going well until my trike got an air lock and broke-down; The fibreglass three-wheelers were renowned for breaking-down. I groaned at my bad luck. Then, Linda's vehicle broke-down. Fortunately, passing drivers were able to help us on the road again.

We took a wrong turn and got lost for a while. Eventually we reached the Rufus stone in the New Forest, which is where we had intended. We drove to Winchester for our stay in the Youth Hostel. Not very accessible, but we managed.

I saw the school consultant and he was very worried about the lack of circulation in my right leg. I went into the local hospital for an operation to hopefully improve this. I went back to school to recuperate during the summer term, hating the big scar across the right side of my stomach. But having the operation did help for many years to come.

The school decided that I didn't have to take end of term exams as I was leaving and couldn't finish the course.

I felt ready to leave.

The school was organising a trip to the House of Commons. I so wanted to go, but I had not long come out of hospital. Hoping for the best, I said that I would be fine, and joined the group. I enjoyed the day but it proved to be a real struggle, I really wasn't ready for such outings for a while. When the consultant came for one of his regular visits, he ordered me back to bed.

We discussed future careers, but any imaginative ideas I came up with were squashed. I agreed to attend a two-year secretarial course at the local college in Taunton with the idea of working in an office.

So it was goodbye to school.

Florence Treloar School had helped me in so many ways. I'd enjoyed many amazing new experiences; I'd taken on responsibilities, and I gained confidence; I was more used to socialising and I'd enjoyed the company of other girls and the various events we participated in.

A little part of me was sad to be leaving.

My parents arrived and loaded their car with my belongings. I had to drive my three-wheeler back home from Hampshire to Somerset by following my parents. These vehicles weren't reliable and my parents drove back very slowly, they were worried. They didn't want to lose me after my two years away from home.

CHAPTER 40

COLLEGE DAYS

I knew I'd become a very different person; two years away from home had taught me to be more self-reliant, more positive in what I wanted to achieve, and more able to communicate. I was still lacking in confidence, but I had taken my first steps towards this. The world was opening up for me.

My parents, on the other hand, wanted to treat me just the same as before – as a child. They couldn't see that I'd changed. I used to be the meek and mild child who'd rather be invisible than cause an argument. It was not long before my mother said 'You're not the nice child you used to be.' As it happens, that rather pleased me.

I was adamant I wanted to give up piano lessons. It had been a chore for so long. My mother said this was too late, she'd already agreed with the piano teacher that it would be her last lesson for that day, and then my father would drive her home. I couldn't win; I grudgingly carried on. I didn't care if I made mistakes, and didn't practise. I tried to ignore it. Eventually the elderly piano teacher retired.

I now had a means of escape with my very own blue Noddy car. I could drive to college, go shopping and meet up with friends. Life was improving.

I turned up for my first day at the local college. My course was taking place on the first floor so I had two lots of staircases to climb, there was no lift. My wheelchair stayed on the first floor.

I'm not sure how I managed to climb those stairs every day, just sheer determination I think. I was so worried that the other students might bump into me and send me flying, either walking or climbing the stairs. I often stopped and hung onto the banister rail as they ran past me. In wet weather, the stairs could be slippery. I had a shoulder-bag full of books to carry as well. Coming down the stairs was even worse: I came down frontwards. I had to drop one leg down to the next step hoping that it landed on that step, lean on my stick to twist enough to drop the other leg. Each step was done with precision, and no-one had any idea just how difficult it was for me. I did that most weekdays for nearly two years.

I had left behind an accessible school designed and built to meet the needs of disabled people. Now I was back in the real world where nothing was accessible.

When were people going to wake up to the fact that disabled people didn't want to be sent away? They wanted to be part of the community.

When were things going to change! When disabled people challenged the system, the public often complained; their thinking was that we should be grateful for what we had.

I gradually got to know the other girls in the class, and over the two years we had some really good times together.

Some of the girls have become good friends for the rest of my life.

Most of the girls went to the canteen for lunch while I mostly stayed upstairs with a packed lunch. Every so often I decided to climb down the stairs and walk to the canteen to join in. It was nice to spend some leisurely time together, but I had to leave early for the walk back with another haul up the stairs.

I remember some of us went to the pub nearby for a drink to celebrate my birthday. We were all pretending to be sober as the girls tried to heave me up the stairs for the afternoon lessons. I could see our tutor was puzzled by our spasmodic bursts of giggles and hiccups in class for the remainder of that college day.

I joined the Rangers, as I wanted to finish my Gold Duke of Edinburgh's Award. I saw Gill from my class at college and we had some fun times together. I also met Jane at Rangers, and we became good friends. There was a Wimpy Bar in town, many of us gathered there in the evenings, after various sessions, to socialise. As I parked alongside, I'd be greeted by the girls and invited to join in.

Sometimes an over-enthusiastic friend would swing my sliding door back with such force, the door would shoot off its slot onto the road. The fibre glass door was so flimsy. I often drove home with the door tied to the roof of the vehicle. Frequently I'd leave a message on the kitchen table for my father: 'Please could you put the door back on my three-wheeler before leaving for work?'

Occasionally in the evenings, I drove a friend back to their home. I only had the one seat for me, and a space at the side for my wheelchair, which I didn't always take. The friend sat on the floor and peered out of the window to give me instructions. If I saw a policeman, I pushed her head down with an elbow. I didn't want to get into more trouble!

Our Ranger Leader asked for volunteers to camp at a Scout Jamboree for a weekend, to help out. I agreed to go along with Gill and some other Rangers. I worked in the refreshment tent on that occasion. We had three tents for sleeping in; the Ranger Leader slept in the middle on her own to keep an eye on us.

We were invited to a social get-together at the local pub. We waited until we heard snoring coming from the middle tent, and then crept out to the pub. It was upstairs, but I was soon lifted up to join everyone. We had a great time and drank far more than we should have. We giggled as we tried to get back into the tent and sleeping bag later that night with only our torches to guide us. Our Leader had trouble getting us to look respectable and follow orders the next day.

I finished my Gold Duke of Edinburgh's Award and received an invitation to Buckingham Palace for the Gold Award, to be presented (of course) by Prince Phillip himself. There were five Rangers in our group along with our parents and our Ranger Leader. It was a very grand occasion. As I couldn't climb the stairs, I was taken to another area to use a lift and we walked through many splendid, impressive corridors to get to the function room. A really memorable occasion for me.

I constantly had problems with my three-wheeler. The fibreglass soon cracked. They weren't really road-worthy, but I was so glad I had one. If it rained, I often had to put an umbrella up in the car as it leaked. It often broke down and I had to ask all sorts of people to help me including, once, the manager of a bank. Traffic wardens often had to push-start me to get the vehicle going again. There were, of course, no mobile phones around at that time to phone for help.

One day I was driving home and had to stop behind a car waiting to turn right. The car behind me hadn't noticed and ploughed into the back of me. My three-wheeler turned upside down and the fibre glass split in two, completely wrecked. Fortunately, I was unhurt, except for some whiplash. I'd demonstrated perfectly how flimsy these cars were. I was given a second-hand three-wheeler while it was sorted out.

Eventually the Ministry stopped making these vehicles in 1977 and started a mobility scheme where disabled people were given an allowance to help them adapt, and use, mainstream cars. I'd looked for my own car to drive a few years before that.

I still had problems finding clothes to fit over my spinal brace and callipers. I bought a sewing machine and operated the foot pedal with my elbow. I often visited the fabric stall at the cattle markets on Saturdays. It was so nice to be able to choose my own fabrics. I spent my free time making clothes, but it wasn't an easy task, as I had to alter many of the patterns. I appreciated how my mother had felt when she'd struggled to make me clothes.

Clothes were becoming more available and cheaper, and so many girls started buying readymade clothes. I'd never bought my own clothes before. I saw a lovely pair of trousers to buy but didn't have the confidence to buy them. I asked my mother if she would come with me but she said 'No', she was too busy. I realised I was on my own and went back to buy them, which was probably the best thing for me.

I was 21. My parents gave me a choice of a birthday present: I could have a party, or a piano. I didn't want either. I didn't understand why I couldn't choose for myself, but it wasn't an option.

The thought of having a party freaked me out; I wasn't ready for a party. The other option, a piano... I had virtually given up playing by then.

We went to buy a piano. As we looked at them in the shop, my parents suddenly asked me whether I was certain. I thought it was a bit late, maybe they'd picked up on my lack of enthusiasm. I just wanted it over and done with and so I said 'Yes'. It was a lovely piano and looked nice in the lounge but there it stayed, even when I moved out. I did eventually sell it and had the money to spend.

I saw my consultant, Mr Hedley Hall, in Bath for the last time, as I was now an adult. He emphasised that I needed to get on with life and make the most of what I could do. It was quite sad, I'd known him ever since I'd contracted polio. He'd offered help and advice so many times. There was now an orthopaedic department in our local hospital so I didn't have to travel further afield.

Towards the end of my two years at college my mother stressed that it would probably take me longer to get a job than most young people, and suggested that I should start applying for jobs before the end of the secretarial course.

I applied for a secretarial job in the Engineering Department at the local hospital. I had an interview, and was offered the job. I couldn't believe that I had the first job I'd applied for. Like my mother, I also thought it would be a struggle.

I returned to the college and explained that I needed to leave before the end of the course because I had a job.

I was the first student in my class to get a job. It made me feel good.

At home, things started to change. Soon after I started to work, my mother got a job. To begin with, she worked a few evenings a week for a security firm. They picked her up and she spent the evening making-up wage packets. If any money was left over, they had to start again, so there was no telling when my mother might return.

Then my mother worked at the local post office a few days a week. She'd always been good with finance. My mother carried on working for quite a few years. The location was ideal because my mother didn't drive.

CHAPTER 41

STARTING WORK

My office building was in a Nissan hut in the grounds of the local hospital. There were a number of Nissan huts around us for the maintenance team, who worked with us. This included engineering, electrical, carpentry and plumbing work. I received phone calls from the hospital wards saying that certain repairs needed to be made, and I had to contact the relevant team. My salary was £15 per week and I gave some of it to my parents. Other duties included typing, photocopying and making tea.

It was a steep learning curve for me. I didn't dare tell them we'd only just got a phone at home, and I jumped every time the phone rang. I dreaded having to take shorthand as the Group Engineer dictated letters to me. My shorthand wasn't brilliant and I tried to memorise as much as I could.

Every Friday I walked to the Finance Department to pick up the cash salaries in a case for the maintenance employees. They would clip a chain from the case to my wrist. I walked back to the office where I locked the door and opened the hatch to hand out the money to the workforce.

Eighteen months later, engineering departments from surrounding hospitals were to be combined with headquarters at Sandhill Park Hospital, not far from town. Sandhill Park was then a large residential home for people with learning disabilities. As with most disabled people at the time, they were separated from mainstream life.

We were allocated a temporary office on the ground floor, and I was asked to go ahead and sort out the filing. I knew that eventually the offices would be moving upstairs, with no lift.

I started applying for different jobs and, in December of 1972, I began working for the Local Government in the Health Department at County Hall. This was situated on the third floor with a lift, which worked most of the time! I shared an office with Pam, doing clerical work.

On the day I started work there, I tried to park my Noddy car outside County Hall, but all the parking spaces nearby were full. The only available space was for the Chief Executive right outside the entrance. I decided that would have to do. Later, some very flustered officials came to explain that I couldn't park there. I virtually said, *Tough, he can walk.* Where was *I* going to park?

Miraculously, they quickly found me a space. I think they were a little annoyed that a humble Noddy car had dared to take the Chief Executive's spot.

I settled into work. With Pam and me in our small office, our bosses shared another small room next door. At Christmas, we had a few decorations to put up. One year Pam locked the office door while she was on a chair putting up our decorations, then we got on with our work. During the morning, we wondered why people were coming to our office, turning the knob, but didn't come in. At lunchtime we realised we hadn't unlocked the office door. No-one had bothered us. We laughed and said we ought to do it more often, but of course we never did.

From January to March 1974, the Government limited the use of electricity because of various strikes. All our typewriters were manual, but we weren't allowed to put the electric light on or have any heating. We needed to work for as long as possible to get as much done as we could. When the light grew dim, our boss knocked on the wall next to our office, which meant we could stop working and go home.

In 1974 the Health Department was divided up. The Scientific Services Department was established and within that role was the Animal Health Service, which is where I would be working. My role changed many times but I continued to work full-time in the Animal Health section for 18 years. I issued licences for pig-keeping, I was involved with the sheep dipping administration, plus I carried out all kinds of other jobs involving animals.

I worked with many different people over the years and they became good friends, and we have been on holidays together. We meet up socially for birthdays and special occasions. I can remember some Christmas work socials where I became a bit tipsy – drinking *much* more than was good for me. But I survived to tell the tale.

Working on the top floor did cause a problem if there were any fire alarms – how to get me down the stairs and out of the building without using the lift. The stairs were far too steep for me to manage. We had a wheelchair which could climb down stairs, but this was a lengthy process. Then we were issued with a chair which looked like a sedan chair, carried by one person in front and another behind. It was never easy. Often, the lift was out of action: I could get to the second floor in another building, but had to have help up to the top floor.

Soon after I started work at County Hall I bought my very first second-hand adapted car from another disabled person. I had driven for seven years on a provisional licence, but like everyone else, I had to take a driving test. I needed to buy the car first and then have lessons, as none of the cars for learners were adapted. I passed and was so pleased to say goodbye to my three-wheeler. It had given me my independence, but just hoped that this new car would be more reliable.

There were so many memorable moments to mention at work. I arrived at work one day to find the tyres of my wheelchair slashed. I reported it and my wheelchair was taken away for repair. Later that day someone mentioned to me that an older man had been noticed fiddling around with my wheelchair. I suddenly remembered that I'd asked my father to pump-up the tyres for me sometime. He had come to the office, unbeknown to me, and pumped them up so high the tyres had split. I had to apologise and admit it was probably my father who'd been the culprit.

Once, there was a loud bang in the office and some postcards flew off the wall behind me. It was assumed to be connected to a crack in the wall. Various people came to inspect the wall and test it with equipment to check the wall was safe. It was only as I prepared to go home I realised that the tyres of my folded wheelchair parked nearby had exploded, creating the bang we'd all heard. It was not the wall at all. The minute crack in the wall had probably been there for years.

I still had to manage my brace and callipers. If a strap broke, I was often stuck. I had to attend the hospital to get it repaired, it took ages and often came back wrong. I sometimes drove to the appliance centre in Exeter to get my brace repaired. The centre was in a shabby barn in the corner of the hospital grounds, almost forgotten.

At best, my brace and callipers never fitted perfectly and I was always adding extra padding to stop my skin from rubbing and hurting. I continued to have painful chilblains in the winter and at times they broke to become ulcers. The ulcers took years to heal and were so painful, but I took painkillers and carried on working.

There were still more operations over the years, to enable me to have as much mobility as possible. My ankle was fixed so that I could continue to walk, so I was in plaster for three months. I had an operation to improve the circulation of my left leg and help heal the leg ulcer after many years of pain. My toes curled under and hindered my walking, so I needed an operation to straighten them. I coped with this and full-time work, often going to work with my leg in plaster.

CHAPTER 42

STRETCHING MY WINGS

I was working and I had a social life but I was still living at home. My parents and I got on fairly well but we weren't close. We were polite with one another, not wanting to say or do anything to upset the situation. I had learnt the art of agreeing with my mother, whether or not I thought she was right or wrong, and it worked. She couldn't start an argument. My father had done this for years to keep the peace but I had struggled with the concept. Now I was older, I understood.

My mother still wanted to be in control, and mentioned that she had every right all the while I was living in their home. It gave me the incentive to move but there was a lack of suitable, available properties. There was still no requirement to build any accessible homes.

My friend, Ann, who had also contracted polio as a child, had married Brad, also disabled, and moved to Taunton and they now lived in a small flat, not accessible but manageable. I often visited them but it was not easy to invite them back home. There was nowhere to sit in my bedroom and my mother took over any conversation in the lounge.

In the meantime, I wanted to go out and explore. I bought disability magazines for inspiration. There was no such thing as the internet at that time.

I read about a disability conference in Holland and applied for a place, and attended. Then I heard about a disability conference in Iran, and I joined the English group and flew via Jordan to Iran.

We stayed in a huge tented campsite just outside Tehran at the base of the Alborz Mountains. There were many groups of disabled people attending from various countries to discuss disability issues. Some countries didn't send any disabled people because they said they had no disabled people – they were not recognised.

We had the chance to explore the capital city of Tehran. It was extremely hot as we joined the bustle in the busy centre. I had to get my wheelchair over the open gullies to cross the roads. We stopped to buy an ice-cream and were immediately ushered into a small back room to join other people also eating ice cream; we hadn't realised that no-one is allowed to eat on the streets.

We visited the Sepahsalar Mosque, a beautiful and historic building. We also visited Golestan Palace, once a Royal Palace built when Tehran had a walled city; and the Palace of Qajar, another important historical building. Towards the end of our stay there we had a visit from the wife of the Shah of Iran who came around and shook each of us by our hand.

After a week in this campsite we travelled by coaches across the desert to another campsite in the middle of nowhere. On the way, we stopped at Qom, considered a holy place, to be shown around the important and amazing mosque. We travelled into Isfahan to learn about the important culture and craft workmanship and visited another impressive mosque. Our English group was invited to the English Embassy, where we had cucumber sandwiches on the lawn, and briefly met the Duchess of Kent on a short visit. We weren't used to the local food and devoured the sandwiches; we were hungry, and grateful for food that we knew. Although we were offered great hospitality, we found the food difficult. Breakfast was naan bread and black tea, and the same for lunch. Our main meal was rice with a mixture of some unknown food, probably vegetables, and sometimes some meat.

I heard of another holiday organisation called the Winged Fellowship Trust, who organised holidays for disabled people, complete with a helper. I looked forward to receiving their list of destinations each year. My first trip was to France along with a group of disabled people from France and Germany and we stayed in Bordeaux.

One evening while in France our van stalled across an unmarked level crossing in the middle of the countryside. Everyone who could get out pushed while the driver tried to start the van. We all sighed with relief as we drove off the tracks. Within minutes of doing that, a high speed train shot by.

Definitely one of my lives used!

I went on safari to Kenya with the Winged Fellowship Trust. Our group of about twenty people loaded three safari buses and headed south to Amboseli National Park. The local tribes people waved and we waved back. The scenery was so spectacular; I heard someone say they could see Mount Kilimanjaro. I looked in the same direction but I couldn't see it. I gradually raised my eyes up to the clouds, then above the clouds, and I gasped as I realised just how close we were. The snow-capped volcano was above the clouds and stood tall and majestic. I felt I could touch it.

We left early every morning for a safari as the sun rose to watch the animals feed. We returned for breakfast but were soon on the safari trail again with Mount Kilimanjaro as our backdrop. The lodges we stayed in were ideal.

We moved on to Tsavo West National Park. Our accommodation was raised off the ground so we could view our surroundings, but it had rained and the animals were hard to see. A leopard visited most evening to eat meat put in a tree.

We spent a week in a beachside hotel with no transport. We met some young men on the beach who offered to take us for trips out. Yes, they said, they could get a bus. We agreed and gave them a small deposit. The receptionists at the hotel shook their heads at us, doubtfully – but the hotel options were too expensive for us. We decided to take a chance. The young men weren't allowed onto the hotel grounds, so at six in the morning we wondered if we had made a mistake as we walked to the local village.

There was a bus, a tatty bus with seats that rattled, but it *was* a bus. We were all loaded onto the bus and the wheelchairs put into a truck behind. The villagers pushed the bus to help start it and the driver turned up the volume of the Reggae music. We were off, with children hanging on for a free ride until we increased our speed.

After a few hours, we reached a small village beside the sea. They had organised a sailing trip on a Dhow. It was a challenge getting us all down the slippery jetty steps but there was plenty of willing hands. We sailed to a tiny idyllic island with a coral reef. Adorned with snorkel gear, I was lowered over the boat into the sea and one of the crew swam with me over the coral reef and pointed out the various fish. I saw parrot fish, angel fish and trumpet fish with such lovely bright colours. To get back on board it was a case of everyone leaning over the boat and getting hold of a part of me to haul me onboard.

Back in the village, we tucked into our barbecue of Barracuda steaks, mince and squid with coconut and rice and a variety of dishes bought at a market on the way and cooked by the villagers. They looked on, probably hoping that we might leave them something to eat later on. Buoyed by this success, we booked some more trips and had a thoroughly good time.

We had another lovely holiday, in Sri Lanka. My friend Izzy came to help me. We boarded small tuk-tuks to get around. Izzy helped to lift me onto the seat and as she climbed on, she collapsed the manual wheelchair and lifted it across us at the back as we set off. On one occasion, the driver took us in the wrong direction and we wondered where we were going to end up. He stopped by a hedge with other tuk-tuks in the middle of nowhere. He picked up his young daughter from school and she sat on his lap as we drove back to our hotel. All was well.

We had a coach trip up to the tea plantations high in the hills of Sri Lanka and watched the women work in the cooler air.

We went to an elephant refuge in a quiet secluded spot by a river, and later on in another area we had a ride on an elephant. I was hauled up a ladder somehow, and sat on sacks with posts tied together, with about eight other people. My lack of balance proved a problem as the elephant moved, so I was tied to one of the posts and it worked. We spent two hours plodding through jungle and swamp. To be free on an elephant was truly exhilarating.

Life was becoming exciting and I relished it.

CHAPTER 43

My Own Flat

I was sitting in the lounge with my parents one evening when my father showed me a page of the local paper he was busy reading. A Housing Association announced they were about to build some one-bedroom flats in another part of Taunton. Without any hesitation, I wrote to the address shown.

I had a quick reply, and to my delight they had agreed to me renting a flat. I was so *excited*. I could have the first ground floor flat with the shortest route to the block of garages. They did state that it was an ordinary flat with no adaptations, and I had to accept it on those terms.

I was determined to manage whatever the problem, and agreed. The flats were ready in February 1978. Just at that time my mother caught shingles and felt poorly so couldn't help, but I had help from friends. Social Services agreed to build a temporary wooden ramp, which stayed in place for ten years.

A lot of furniture came from home. The settee I had spent so many years sitting on came with me, along with an old sideboard and a cupboard for my television. My parents still watched their black and white television, but I decided to rent a colour television, still relatively new; they were too expensive to buy at that time. What a difference it made to viewing! Everything came to life.

My bed came too, and bedside cabinet. There was already an inbuilt wardrobe. The kitchen was so small the freezer had to go into my bedroom.

The bathroom was my main problem. The bathroom door was narrower than the rest of the doorways. I had to take off my callipers and spinal brace to have a bath, and the wheelchair would not fit through the door. I obtained a smaller wheelchair which I squeezed into when I wanted a bath.

I had to prove that I could manage.

It was a steep learning curve. I had to run a home, work full-time and cater for myself. I had never shopped for food, and for a while meals were a bit haphazard. My mother agreed to continue with my washing as there was no room for a washing machine. We weren't allowed to hang washing outside, also none of the laundry facilities were accessible. I really appreciated my mother's help, but it still gave her a hold on me.

Shopping was a problem. I used a stick in each hand to help me walk, so I couldn't hold a shopping basket. If I used my manual wheelchair in town, I had to negotiate kerbs to cross roads. There were no out-of-town supermarkets, just in town. I managed somehow and bought small quantities each time in order to cope.

I didn't find it easy to wheel myself around the uneven town centre, and usually walked, choosing a small area to concentrate on where I could buy most things. I had to be careful when walking. The pavements became slippery after rain, and either my stick slipped or my foot, and I would land in a heap, having to ask to be hauled up by passers-by. Autumn leaves were a big problem, and icy areas in winter. People walking by could accidentally knock me over, as my balance was poor; I had to be constantly aware of this possibility. Sometimes I stopped walking and braced myself if I thought it might happen. Everything took much longer than anyone else could imagine.

I loved being in my own flat. But the mind can do funny things: I'd always felt that as I hadn't been able to say goodbye to either my mother or my brother, they were still around haunting me. I imagined them both sitting side by side on the settee looking at me; like ghosts, appearing hideous, showing the awfulness of how they'd died. Scary. I didn't want to see them, so would never go into the lounge in the dark. While living with my parents I had to make sure that their lounge door was shut before going to bed. In my first flat, this image had followed me. When dark, I always made sure I put the light on first before going in, and if passing the open door, I never looked in. Then I moved to the bungalow and once again the image followed me. Sometimes I felt brave enough to enter in the dark, but never looked at the settee. I had accepted that the image would stay with me forever. Many years later, while Tim and I were away with some good friends, I felt comfortable enough to tell them. As soon as I told them, it was as if by magic that the image receded. *The power of sharing a problem!* I thought people would laugh, but no-one did. It made me realise what a difference it would've made to have told someone earlier, but who to tell? The image is still there in my memory but now I feel it's no threat.

Now, in my flat, I could invite friends around as well as visit them. The friends I'd made at Camp came from all over England and I often travelled by train to visit them for the weekend and they came to stay with me.

When I travelled by train I had to sit in my wheelchair in the guard's van along with parcels, bags of post, bicycles and any other luggage thrown in. None of the carriages were accessible. There was no heating, no access to food and no toilets of any kind. I sat for hours in the cold knowing that I couldn't drink, watching the deliveries come and go. I paid the same fare as everyone else. If anyone came along with me, they had to sit on the floor or perch on whatever was in the guard's van.

It was worth putting myself through this, as I really enjoyed being with my friends and the things we did together.

I had various experiences with the train service over many years. On one occasion, Rachael and I were travelling in the Guard's van to Gatwick Airport. We waited at one station for ages. A guard appeared and looked surprised to see us. He told us that the train had broken down. An announcement had been made, and everyone transferred. Of course, there were no announcements in the guard's van. The guard said they were just about to shift the train and coaches to a siding. I dread to think what could've happened to us. It was still years before mobile phones.

I was travelling back from the North of England by myself, and was told by the station porters that the train was late. I asked if there was time for me to pop to the toilet, as I knew there were no accessible toilets on the train. When I returned they looked at me in horror, the train had come and gone. It was the last train. They made some quick phone calls and I had various trains stopping at unscheduled stops to get me back to Taunton that evening.

On another occasion, I arrived at Taunton station to be told that the lift to the platform I needed was broken. They decided to take me up in another lift to the next platform along and then diverted the train to that platform. They made an announcement, and a lot of people complained as they rushed over to the platform I was on. I kept quiet, of course.

Now the trains are accessible. It is lovely to be able to sit along with everyone else in the warm with an accessible toilet nearby. What a difference this makes.

A local PHAB Club started where disabled people and non-disabled people could socialise together. I met up with Lynne again and her husband Roger. Lynne and I had lived next-door to each other for many years in Trull, and as children we attended the same Guide company for a while. We rekindled our friendship. It turned out that we lived quite near each other.

Our PHAB group organised many social trips. I had the chance to abseil down Cheddar Gorge, so a small group of us set off to meet our instructors. We arrived at the bottom of the cliff and looked up. I thought we would arrive at the top of the cliff to abseil down. The instructors said that we all had to get to the top of the cliff first. How was I going to do that?

We put our gear on and then everyone took a piece of me and they climbed up the cliff hauling me up behind them over bulky boulders. My wheelchair came as well. Once over the edge of the cliff in my wheelchair abseiling down, I realised that my safety helmet was really heavy and dragged my head backwards. I had never realised that my neck muscles were weak. I couldn't see what I had to do, so relied on the instructor coming down beside me. It was an interesting experience seeing the world upside down while trying to come down a cliff face.

I went to London with friends to see London shows. The theatres did their best with old buildings to make it as accessible as possible, but we had some odd experiences. Jane and I went to see Phantom of the Opera and we had to lean around a pillar to see the stage. Liz and I went to see Les Miserables; we had our own box, but had to crouch down to see all the stage.

The best experience was when a friend and I went to see Mutiny on the Bounty starring David Essex. We followed a member of staff down a side street, where they unlocked a door which led to a box at the side of the stage with a lovely view. At the interval I needed the toilet. We had to retrace our steps to the main entrance and be hauled up the steps to the toilet. On our return, we found the door to our balcony locked. The usher said the person with the key had gone home.

He said to wait a minute, and disappeared.

They came up with a solution. Apparently, someone entered the next box to ours in the theatre and hanging onto the plush curtains, he swung himself from one box to our box and rushed to open the door. This caused quite a stir with the audience, looking at the usher instead of the stage, wondering whether it was all part of the performance. When we entered the box, everyone looked at us. David Essex had competition that day!

I asked Liz if she and Stephanie would come to Norway with me. Stephanie was studying for her GCSEs, but she wanted to come with us. I booked a chalet by a fjord. I drove my car onto the ferry and then to the chalet, trying to stay on the right side on the road. We drove over mountain passes and snow drifts, saw glaciers and ancient churches. The scenery was amazing. The chalet was owned by a cherry farmer and we were allowed to help ourselves to the succulent cherries. The owners took us for a boat trip along the fjord and Stephanie often braved the cold water for a swim.

I changed cars over time with various adaptations to help me drive. I now drive a van in my electric wheelchair with a side lift. It's great to be mobile. I drive all over the place but as I get older I find long distances very tiring. I live in a beautiful part of the country so don't have to go that far to see lovely countryside.

There have been several occasions when the adaptations have decided not to work. One day I drove to a supermarket to do some shopping. Once back in the car park with my van loaded, I backed onto the lift to get into the van. As I reached the top, the lift for some reason just folded up into the van with me still on it. It threw me and the wheelchair backwards. I lay on the floor of the van, stunned. Fortunately, I had landed on a pack of toilet rolls, so the landing was relatively soft. No-one had seen this happen – I was completely on my own. I moved slowly, and realised that I wasn't hurt. Somehow, I managed to get onto the back seat, turn the wheelchair upright, and get back in to reach the driving seat. Luckily, it has never happened since.

Life was a challenge, but I was having fun and times were changing. I could see growing improvements for disabled people – at last.

CHAPTER 44

Pathfinders Friends

I'd known Dorcas from Pathfinders Camp for many years. She is disabled by Cerebral Palsy and uses a wheelchair. She and I met up for weekends in London with our friends. Jill and Jenny usually came along, and sometimes other friends joined us. We explored London, visited museums and went to shows. Dorcas and I even went to Spain for a week's holiday with three friends.

Dorcas is an amazing person, she's been a huge inspiration to me. She has no control over her arms and legs, and types using a pen in her mouth to tap the keyboard, or a brush in her mouth to paint. Despite this, she has represented disabled people on various committees and flown to many countries to attend conferences. She has written numerous books, and has been awarded the MBE for her commitment to promoting rights for disabled people.

I often went to see Jill and John who live in Walsall. I watched their children grow up: Kevin, Helen and Laura. Some people were still cautious of anyone in a wheelchair, but the children were at ease and we had fun together.

Bobby ran the camp for a while and lived in the middle of the Yorkshire Dales. Many of us visited her for weekends, walking the countryside and chatting by the log fire at night.

In 1986, four helpers from Camp agreed to come with me to stay at The Guide Chalet in Switzerland. It was really a walking holiday, but the leader of the Chalet agreed to let me be part of it, and drove me to places to meet up with my friends. I joined in some of the walks, my friends attached a rope to each side of my wheelchair and hung on to it to stop me from rolling away, or just to heave me up a big slope. On one occasion, as I got into the car, my wheelchair took off down a steep hill. Everyone chased after it to try to stop the wheelchair before it crashed or disappeared.

The leader announced that everyone was going by coach to a local town and walk onwards to a glacier. She explained that the terrain was far too difficult for me and my wheelchair, and said that, instead, we could wander around the town. Suddenly, we spotted a bus with *Glacier* displayed as its destination, and we got on board. We got off the bus in the middle of nowhere. We hadn't planned this, it just happened. There was a path leading to the undergrowth with a sign saying 'Glacier'. We set off thinking that the path was quite good, but then it deteriorated. My friends Rose, Pat, Maureen and Nicole got out the ropes and tried to continue. None of us wanted to admit defeat, but it looked likely.

A group of Boy Scout leaders suddenly appeared and they lifted me over the rocks to the glacier. We were at the glacier even before our group had arrived. We set off for our return trip wondering how we were going to cope over the rocky terrain. The wheelchair skidded and feet slipped. *What if we really got stuck?* Then a group of ramblers materialised and lifted me to the better path. What a stroke of luck! We caught the bus back into the town and boarded our coach. We were exhilarated seeing the glacier, but realised how horribly wrong it could've gone.

I started helping with the Trull Guide Company, and then became leader. This took up a lot of my spare time organising Guide evenings, but it proved great fun. We went camping, had weekends in London, discos with the Scouts, and bus trips to Bristol for the ice rink. I had many good helpers with me over the years and continued to run the company for nearly twenty years.

When we went to London, I had to get permission to book the Baden Powell House for Scouts, as the Guide hostel was completely inaccessible to me. We all travelled to London by train and then by Underground to the hostel. I had to do the last stretch by taxi. We explored London, fed the pigeons in Trafalgar Square, and saw two West End shows.

Some Guides became rebellious teenagers as they grew. At one Parade church service it was Mother's Day and the children were encouraged to go to the altar for a posy of flowers for their mother. I hadn't noticed an older girl go to the altar until she returned, kissed me on the cheek, and gave me a bunch of flowers; then returned to the back of the church. I was stunned. It was a lovely gesture from someone who had now matured from her former self as a somewhat wild young girl.

Liz, who I knew from Pathfinders Camp, married Dave and moved into the area. Liz came to help me at Guides. Her daughter Stephanie is my goddaughter. I often went off with them to explore Dartmoor and Exmoor, and their son

Michael in his teenage years pushed me through unmarked paths in the countryside. They were determined that the countryside could become accessible, even though it might be a struggle.

On a different occasion, Liz – never to be beaten – yet again demonstrated what a good friend she is; she hauled me up the theatre steps to see a performance by the New Seekers. She didn't want me to miss out on anything, and I rarely have when I've had my good friends around me.

I owe them so much, and I cherish them all.

Paignton - 1983

High in the rigging - 1983

Sailing on Sealegs - 1986

Rita 'rowing' a dinghy - 1986/87

In Malta - Spring 1989

Riding on an elephant in Sri Lanka - 2000

Rita and Izzy in Sri Lanka - 2000

With a baby lion - 2005

With a cheetah - 2005

Water rafting in Peru - 2006

Bowsprit view - 2006

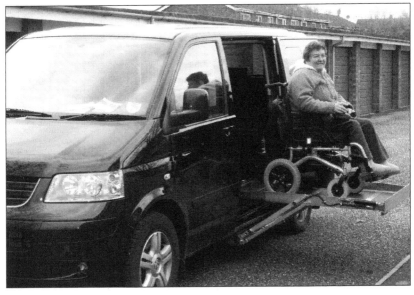

On the lift of my van - 2010

Rita and Tim - Valentine's Day 2017

Feeding Reindeer - Lapland 2019

Sleigh ride - Lapland 2019

CHAPTER 45

ON THE OCEAN WAVE

The Silver Jubilee Sailing Trust wanted to build a sailing ship where disabled people could take a full part in the running of the ship while sailing on the open seas. WOW, I thought, that would be different.

To make sure the project worked, they commissioned the Soren Larsen for three years, a brigantine (a two-masted sailing ship with square-rigged sails on the foremast and fore-and-aft sails on the mainmast) which had just been used for making the television series The Onedin Line. The owner and skipper agreed, and some changes were made to make it feasible.

I applied and got a place on the first ever sailing trip. There was no accessible gangway and anyone who couldn't walk was swung over in a net, and the wheelchair carried over. I signed on as a member of the crew to sail for the next 10 days. I knew Peter and Simon, who had come along with me.

There was a permanent crew of six and then a mixture of able and disabled people. Some people had sailing experience and others, including me, had none. We were split into four watches and I was assigned to the Aft Starboard team with about ten other people. We listened to the instructions we needed to know for our part of the ship. I tried to remember the names of the ropes we needed to use. We did an emergency drill and practised putting on life jackets.

Our Aft Starboard team worked with the Aft Port team. To turn direction of the ship at sea, we pulled on ropes while the Aft Port team let loose and vice versa to turn another way. I had the Top Gallant rope to pull the highest, smallest mast but we all had to help heave on the heavier ropes, especially if there was a strong wind. The four teams worked on a rota system. When we were on watch we were given specific duties for the allocated time with the occasional 'All hands on deck!' when everyone needed to handle the ropes to change direction.

The next morning, we climbed into our wet weather gear. There was a gale blowing, just what we needed to get our sea legs with an incoming tide as we tried to motor out. It was too rough to put any sails up. The ship rolled around in the rough sea and I wondered if I'd made the right decision to come as we staggered around the ever-moving deck. In the afternoon, our watch was on duty. At first, I was put on look-out to make sure we knew about any other ships or boats in the area, and then I was asked to go on the helm.

An old dentist chair had been secured in place so that I could be transferred and work the wheel. It took a lot of concentration to try to keep the wheel at a certain compass point, the sea was so rough. From the helm, towards the back of the ship, I could see the full length of the ship as it lurched forward and pitched into the next large wave. The ship shuddered as the large waves smashed into the front of the ship, sending spray over everyone.

I glanced at the skipper, who seemed quite calm. He noticed that I had gone quite pale and sent me down to the main deck which did not roll so much. We could hear continuous crashes and bangs coming from the kitchens – until the cook gave up and came out to sit down.

The skipper decided to alter course for Studland Bay, and shelter for the night. We were soon hungry and discussed the day's events at the bar. I went to sleep with the creaking wood of the old ship as we rolled gently in the sheltered bay.

The next day was no better as we battled against the wind and tide. We could not cross the sea but tacked our way along the coast to the safety of Weymouth. We had to spend three days stuck in Weymouth until the gale subsided. We had a daily session of Happy Hour to keep the ship clean.

One of the crew walked by with large pot of tallow to brush onto the main mast to keep it smooth for hauling up the collar of the gaff, which pulls up the main mast. I said 'Can I have a go?' He said 'I don't see why not.' The next thing I knew was that I was getting in a boiler suit and being winched up the 60 ft mast to help to tallow it. What an experience – and what a view! The JST wanted to make sure everyone was included and the crew were doing just that.

The skipper announced that if we left harbour early the next day, we could sail across the channel to Cherbourg before the next low. We were ready.

We woke to a clear blue sky, and unfurled the sails as we left the harbour. As we reached the open sea, the wind filled the sails as we worked on the ropes listening to instructions. There was still a strong wind and 8 foot waves, which crashed into the side of the ship causing a heavy sway, but everyone was in good spirits as we sailed along.

With the engine off and all the sails up, all we could hear was the sound of the waves as the wind blew us along.

It was magical.

There was no land in sight. For lunch we had a snack of rolls, cheese and salad. This is what I had come for.

Large waves frequently crashed over the side of the ship, soaking anyone who happened to be there or walking by at the time. There was no knowing where or when the next wave would hit the ship, so we just had to take our chances. I was wearing my wet weather gear and had been strapped to the side of the ship to stop me moving. I was in my element. Then I noticed this very large wave approaching my side of the ship. There was nothing I could do, it all happened so quickly. A deluge of water soaked me totally. I felt like I needed to come up for air.

The fun was trying to get me below and changed with the swaying of the ship. Everyone was finding it difficult to balance, which made the job twice as long as we tried to support one another. Everyone was laughing and joking, it was a great atmosphere as we rolled along.

We couldn't dock alongside in Cherbourg, so dropped anchor just outside. We had a leisurely day and we were lowered into the small rubber dinghy to go ashore. The wheelchairs were heaved over first, and then us. Those who could walk climbed down the ladder. From the harbour we looked out to sea and saw our ship. Had we just sailed over in her?! She looked beautiful. I was very proud of her, and of myself.

We sailed back through the night. I put on as many layers of clothing as I could to work with my watch. As we sailed into the dark, the coastline was dotted with lighthouse lights, each with their different signals to keep ships safe. It was a whole new experience looking for the right rope to pull in the dark as we followed orders to set the braces for sail.

The wind force was 5 and we surged ahead with the wind behind us. It was late when I took a turn at the helm. Those not on duty had gone to bed. It was so quiet; just a few lights to alert other ships. It was a clear night and I had never seen so many stars dotting the sky. I felt that it was just me and the ship.

It seemed as though we needed to whisper in order not to break the silence. At midnight my duty was over, and bed beckoned. I was so tired I just collapsed onto bed and woke up with my hat still on and salt crystals on my face.

The following morning we tacked along the coast to get back to Southampton. By now we were all one big family, including the crew who had helped us to experience so much. That was *it*, gales or no gales, I was hooked.

As soon as I got home, I said to Ann, you just have to come: no excuses accepted, and we went together the next year. We sailed to Cherbourg again and this time docked alongside the harbour wall. We had arrived during a festival and before we knew what was happening, we were being pushed along the streets holding a lantern trying to sing French songs. We ended up in a bar where we sang a mixture of French and English songs, singing the night away. There were quite a few sore heads the next day, including mine. When we returned home, Ann immediately booked another sailing trip. We had both become addicted to sailing and went on many sailing trips together.

The JST realised that the project would be a great success and started to build the Lord Nelson, a purpose-built ship, accessible for all disabled people. It was a challenge we could all enjoy.

CHAPTER 46

SAILING ON 'SEA LEGS'

'Sea Legs' is a 30ft catamaran which had been slightly adapted to take a disabled person as part of a small team. Could I get a team together? I asked Peter, who was an experienced sailor, and Graham who also sailed. I asked Rachael at work, she had never sailed before but was happy to give it a go. The RYA provided a qualified person to come with us.

There was a ramp to get on board the outside of the catamaran, but the door into the boat was narrow, so I needed to get onto the floor and shuffle inside and everywhere inside the boat. The boat was quite compact so most things were within reach. The toilet was at the front of the boat. I had to get onto a seat called the 'Thunderbox Flyer'. The legs were on wheels set in a groove and when on the seat I glided along the aisle and into the toilet area. This did cause chaos when at sea. Sometimes I would emerge from the toilet only for the boat to tilt on the next wave to send me back again, or I would rush down to the toilet as the boat hit a wave and have to hang on. Equally, I could leave the toilet area and shoot down to the door. All a bit hairy; I just hoped no-one was in the way. The name seemed very apt.

We set sail in a choppy sea and landed a few hours later on the Isle of Wight. Rachael felt fine until she had to disappear inside to the toilet. As we went for a meal in a pub, we left Rachael wandering up and down the quay holding a biscuit. She still felt positive as we set sail the next day. On our first trip, we managed to sail to France.

On the second trip, the weather was too rough out at sea so we sailed locally. We sailed up the river Hamble and moored by a pub for the night; we also sailed up the Beaulieu River and visited Bucklers Hard Maritime Museum. We spent the evening at the pub there. Peter noticed a public phone in the corner and went off to phone his wife. The rest of the group followed. I was the only one who hadn't used the phone, so decided to phone my parents and say Hi. I got through to my mother, who said immediately:

'What's wrong?'

'Nothing's wrong,' I replied. Before I could say any more, my mother continued:

'Then why waste money on a phone call!' and she put the phone down. Well, I'd tried. I did feel rejected but there again, I didn't usually phone home. I went back and said they were out. As we walked back to the boat for the night, we heard the landlord run after us, shouting. We each looked guilty wondering which of us had forgotten to pay. He gave us the loaf of bread we had bought from him and left behind.

I can remember a couple of incidents while sailing on the catamaran. When we were not needed, we relaxed on the front of the boat pretending we were the owners. One day as we crossed the Solent, we both sat at the front of the boat leaning on the rail with our feet over the edge. A ferry crossed in front of us, causing a large wave, which came right over me and soaked me through. Rachael saw it coming and got out of the way quickly, but there was nothing I could do. Another time we were on the front of the boat and the wind picked up one of my socks. I swayed over to try and grab it. Rachael thought I had lost balance and was going overboard. She hung onto me with a tight grip saying 'You're ok, I've got you.' It was good to know I was in safe hands.

There were occasions when we could not moor alongside, so dropped anchor. I was lifted with my wheelchair into the dinghy and we rowed to shore, much to the amusement of passers-by, especially when I decided to have a go at rowing. On one occasion Rachael tried to throw a rope to someone who could guide us to the jetty. It kind of went past the person and hooked round someone's line, a man who was fishing. Did they not know we were novices! Another time we went ashore to buy some fish and chips for supper; Rachael fancied some curry sauce but didn't use it all. She threw the sauce overboard but didn't check on the direction of the wind. In the morning, it looked as though a large seagull had messed all over one side of the boat. The captain was not amused as the scrubbing brushes came out, but we had to laugh.

On one trip we had sailed to Poole and up the river to Wareham to enjoy a festival. It was time for us to sail back from Poole to Lympstone, but the sea was quite rough. We all wore our life jackets. Rachael took some sea-sickness tablets and promptly fell asleep on the bench inside. For more support, I was sitting with my back against the boat and secured to the side. As we reached the open seas, I couldn't believe the height of the waves. I thought each wave was going to swamp us, but it picked up the boat and we soared over the top and down again to the next wave. I found it a bit too scary for comfort. Our captain was in his element: 'Look how fast we're going!' he said.

Rachael awoke and the captain shouted for her to come up on deck. She wanted to sit next to me, but he directed her to sit the other side to even-out the boat. This scared us even more. I was so glad when we reached land, but I have to say I've never forgotten the adrenaline I experienced as we sailed through that rough sea. The catamaran had looked so small battling the elements. I'd spotted another boat just ahead of us making the same journey.

We sailed four times altogether. On the final trip I had my leg in plaster, but not to be defeated, we went ahead. This time we sailed to France, Guernsey, Sark and Alderney. There were no cars in Sark and it was too steep for anyone to push me. There was another boat unloading supplies with a front-loader tractor picking up the supplies. He offered to take me, so I sat in my wheelchair surrounded by frozen vegetables as we went up the hill. There was no problem going down again.

We all had a great time with many memories and lots of laughing. Such a wonderful experience.

CHAPTER 47

A New Home + A Broken Leg

Although I could manage moving around in my small flat, there was very little room if I did use my wheelchair for health reasons or simply because I was tired. I often ached from the effort of walking all the time.

It took me about two hours every morning just to get dressed with my spinal brace and callipers and get ready for work. Then I joined the queue of traffic to travel to work starting at 8.30 a.m. Most mornings I didn't even think about it, I just went through the process. Work gave me the incentive to get up every day, but some days it was definitely a struggle if things didn't go right – like another sore place, a broken strap, or just a heavy cold.

I had been on the Council Housing List for ten years for a more accessible place. In 1988 the Council offered me a newly-built accessible bungalow, and I accepted it. I didn't have to squeeze through the bathroom door anymore. I could move around the kitchen, and there was room for a fridge-freezer and a washing machine. I even had a small garden.

My parents lived nearby and were willing to help. I welcomed the help, but I still wanted to be in control. I came home from work to find notes on the table saying what jobs they had done. A security light suddenly appeared in the carport without me knowing. Fish appeared in the fish pond, as they assumed I wouldn't be able to manage. I just wanted them to communicate with me and find out how they could help me, but they'd been in control for so long, they didn't understand. I had to tread carefully.

I attended a PHAB conference at Manchester University. It poured with rain as we made our way to the bar in the evening. In our hurry to get out of the rain, the front wheel of my wheelchair caught on a cobblestone. The wheelchair stopped but I didn't. I shot forward and landed in a puddle on the ground, and felt my leg break.

I went by ambulance to the Manchester Royal United hospital, where I needed a full-length plaster on the right leg. I had to stay in hospital. My right leg was completely paralysed and now had a very heavy plaster.

I woke early the following morning and saw a telephone coin-operated machine at the end of my bed. I needed to phone my parents and let them know. I wasn't looking forward to it. As expected, my mother picked up the phone, heard my voice, and said 'What's wrong?' I blurted out that I'd broken my leg. 'You stupid girl!' I heard my mother say. That was it; I was already feeling very low. I think my mother realised she needed to change her tone. I can't remember what followed, but they knew exactly how I felt.

I was in the Manchester hospital for a week before an ambulance could be organised to bring me back down to Taunton and my local hospital. That is where I stayed for another three weeks while trying to work out how I was going to manage at home. *Thank goodness I had moved to my bungalow.* At least there would be room to wheel myself around with my leg stuck out in front of me.

I went back to work doing the hours I could. There was no way I could drive. I booked an accessible taxi to get me to work and back. My leg was in plaster all through the summer.

In September, after four months, the plaster was taken away and I was signed-off to go back to work full-time. I thought my problems were over. I thought I would just put my callipers back on and walk again.

By the next morning, my leg had swollen to the size of a football and it was agony just to touch it. I had not expected this. No-one had mentioned that this might happen. My leg was far too swollen to get into the calliper. After taking a lot of pain killers, I just about managed to get into my wheelchair, slide into the car and drag my wheelchair in behind the seat to get to work.

I was in pain all day and every day. I went for physiotherapy, they strapped my leg to a machine to help the swelling, with no real effect. It took two months for the swelling to go down so that I could put my calliper on.

I tried to stand but it was pure agony if I put any pressure on my right leg. I stood for ages, willing myself to shuffle forward a bit, but I just couldn't cope with the level of pain. The heel of my right foot had gone soft and once in the calliper it couldn't cope with any pressure. I tried walking between the parallel bars at physio, but the pain continued and nothing improved. I felt really depressed.

In November, I turned 40, and my very good friends Maggie and Jane organised a surprise birthday party. They called it 'This is your life' and had asked many friends to join in. I even had a birthday cake in the shape of a Tall Ship. It was a lovely surprise and just what I needed.

I was trying to cope and continue working full-time. It took all my effort just to try to get to work in the mornings, so I was always late. Then I had to leave early for physiotherapy appointments. My working hours suffered. My boss eventually mentioned the number of hours I needed to make up and I knew this wasn't possible. I knew I wasn't coping with work. He suggested the possibility of retiring on medical grounds. I felt that I'd tried to cope for long enough, and I agreed. I left the following year.

With no need to work, I put my callipers on and sat in my wheelchair staring at them. I just didn't know what to do. After trying for six months, the pain was no less. I made myself stand up and walk a few feet. Then I stood rooted to the spot while I summed up the courage to get back to my wheelchair.

What was I going to do? I was in no pain until I tried to put any weight on my right leg. I tried and tried with no improvement. It was *so* frustrating. I felt as though my life was on hold.

CHAPTER 48

More Freedom

One morning I woke up and thought: *Maybe I don't have to walk again!* Was that such a bad thing? It would definitely take the pain away and I could start thinking of a way forward. It was a huge decision to make. I had spent my whole life as a disabled person making sure I could walk. It was what my parents had constantly worked towards.

Times were changing. The emphasis was on changing society to make it more accessible for disabled people, not forcing disabled people to walk just to fit in. Wheelchairs were improving; instead of being purely functional, they were now more comfortable and could be adapted to meet the varying needs of disabled people. There was still a long way to go but the improvements were making my life so much easier.

The more I thought about the idea, the more positive I became. I left my callipers under the bed, it meant I could get dressed quicker. I didn't have to worry about altering my trousers or making them to fit over my callipers. I realised how sore the callipers had made me, and this wouldn't be an issue anymore. Without my callipers I found I could relax, they'd made me so constricted.

I told my parents that I was giving up walking, and they were horrified. I was undoing all their hard work over the years. They couldn't appreciate the struggle it had been for me. I realised that it'd take time for them to accept my idea.

I felt liberated and free. I still had to wear a spinal brace but I felt so much better. What was I going to do with my life now? I didn't want to retire from work, I needed to keep active. In September I enrolled on a computer course at college; a lift had been installed, so that was excellent for me.

Computers were the future and I needed to learn.

Since giving up work, I realised how stressed I'd become trying to work full-time, looking after a home and cooking for myself. Everything took longer, and I now had more time to cope. I knew that although I wanted to go back to work, it needed to be part-time. Because I was home, I could employ a cleaner to help me and therefore ease the stress between my parents and me. I felt this change needed to be made.

I was told that finding work was harder after reaching forty. Yet again, I proved people wrong. I was offered a part-time job in the Property Services back in County Hall. After a year, I transferred to a job in the Social Services Department. I then worked for a disability organisation for a few years. I trained to become a Disability Equality Trainer and travelled around Somerset, holding day courses on disability issues. I also taught disability subjects to disabled people at our local college for one day a week. I did this for two years. I met Lynn who was interested in volunteering in the office. We became good friends. I also met Rita around this time, who became another good friend.

Lynn is an Elvis fan and wanted to look around the residential home Gracelands in Memphis. I wanted to see the Mardi Gras Carnival in New Orleans. We joined forces and toured America. While planning the trip I heard about a horse-riding ranch in Arizona which was completely wheelchair accessible, so I contacted them and booked three days while staying in Las Vegas.

I kept this as a surprise for Lynn, so she is now suspicious of any trips I plan. I have no balance, so had to be surrounded by cowboys as we trotted round the paddock, to stop me falling off – well, that's my version! Then they offered Lynn a horse ride and brought out another horse. I thought she too would go around the paddock, but a cowboy appeared on a horse and led Lynn out into the desert of Arizona for a couple of hours. I wondered if Lynn would ever talk to me on her return. I had forgotten to ask if she had ever ridden a horse before. Just once before, I think!

Richard administered a disability organisation and drove an adapted van, and encouraged me to do the same. Pushing a manual wheelchair had become hard work and my shoulders and arms ached from the effort. An electric wheelchair would certainly alleviate this problem. Did this mean I needed to drive a van? It seemed a daunting mission, but seeing how my boss managed, I went ahead with a converted van.

I attended a course in Bristol for disabled people. We were asked to talk about our childhood background. My voice shook as I tried to explain, I hadn't realised just how difficult it was for me to talk about my past. I had never talked about it to anyone. Many other people on the course had traumatic childhood experiences. Somehow, it linked us together.

I met Gina on the course and we often chatted. I asked Gina if she would come to Thailand with me. Up for a challenge, we flew out and joined a group. We wanted to explore more and often took off in tuk-tuks by ourselves. We just pointed to a tuk-tuk and before we knew it, a group of men lifted me and my wheelchair onto the back, and off we went. Of course, we got into a few scrapes. One night we found ourselves walking back to the hotel in the dark in the road against three lanes of traffic because we had run out of good pavement. Some young lads helped us across the road simply by putting their hands up to slow down the traffic; we were so grateful.

We've been on many holidays together since.

Izzy and I had become good friends and we spent a weekend together in Paris. I arranged to travel by Eurostar, booking an assisted place. When the train arrived at the platform, no-one came to assist us. Time passed, most people were on the train; we didn't want to miss it. A waiter noticed our predicament. He shot off the train, grabbed the ramps and ushered us on board.

To our surprise, we had got into luxury first class. We had a luxury meal, with as much wine as we could drink. We were both a bit tipsy as we reached Paris, and had to try and find our way to the hotel.

We visited the Basilica of the Sacred Heart (Sacre Coeur), a famous church built on the top of a hill overlooking Paris. We arrived to find steps up to the church, so Izzy disappeared in with her dictionary of French phrases to see if there was an alternative route. We were directed around the back to a door which was locked. Izzy disappeared again to try to sort this out. I sat outside in the sun when suddenly the door was opened by a nun; she ushered me inside, and locked the door again.

The nun beckoned me to the small lift and showed me which button I needed to press. Once the lift arrived, I realised the door of the lift was behind me and I couldn't open it. I tried to back into the door to try to push the door outwards, but to no avail. I told myself not to panic. I wondered how often the lift was used, and just how long before I was discovered in there. Surely Izzy wouldn't leave without me!

Suddenly the lift moved and shot upwards. Two nuns opened the door, looked surprised, said sorry in French, and tried to shut the door. I grabbed one of their cloaks and hung on. Probably not the done thing but I didn't want to be trapped again. No-one understood English. One nun squeezed into the lift with me and let me out to the cathedral rear door.

How on earth was I going to find Izzy!

As I pushed the rear door to go in, there was Izzy pushing the other door to come out. We sighed with relief that we were together again. It had taken Izzy that long to try to find someone who had understood her.

With this scary incident behind us, we went on to explore Paris and thoroughly enjoyed ourselves.

Izzy and I stayed in Interlaken in Switzerland early one year. We went up the snow-capped mountains by cable car to a spectacular village with foot-high snow on the roofs of the chalets. People moved around on skis, but the road was so packed hard with snow, it was easy to push me through the village – to other people's amazement.

We also flew to Iceland and hired a car for a few days. The insurance only covered us for main roads, but within an hour we'd misread the map and found ourselves heading up and along an unmarked road. The four-wheel drivers eyed us with suspicion as we tried to find our way down again. We drove along the south road to a lake with ice glaciers. Iceland was experiencing a heat wave of nearly 30 degrees centigrade at the time, rarely known in Iceland. It was hot in the hotel and I asked if the rooms had air conditioning; the staff laughed, it wasn't something they usually needed.

We decided to cool off in their swimming pool, but it was hot thermal water. On the plus side, it was nice not to have to wrap up warm while we were there.

CHAPTER 49

I Fall In Love

I had given up on the idea of ever falling in love; that is what happens for other people, not me.

I saw couples enjoying life together. I wondered what would have happened if I hadn't caught polio. My life would've been very different. Hopefully I would have got married, but then no-one ever knows what is ahead of them, disabled or not. I felt my life had been alright, love or no love. I'd made the best of what I had.

In my younger days, it was much harder for disabled people to get married. The general public didn't see many disabled people and were cautious. Everything is so different now, and so much easier. There are so many things we can be open about in life, although there's always room for more improvements. There are far more opportunities for disabled people to socialise and start relationships.

Then I fell in love. I had waited a long time, but it was worth the wait to find the right man.

I was 45 when I met Tim. He lives in Exmouth. I love his twinkling eyes and happy smile. He has a lovely calm soft way of speaking, making me feel safe in his company. We became good friends and we often went out for the day, either in Exmouth or Taunton, enjoying each other's company.

Some friends asked if I would like to go away with them for a weekend. I invited Tim and booked two rooms. We enjoyed the heated indoor swimming pool, Jacuzzi with a hoist, and a large sauna room. I was lying in the sauna room on my front when Tim asked if he could massage my leg. He was doing a massage course at evening class. I was so worried that he might drop my leg afterwards, which would really hurt on the wooden slats; instead, he was really gentle, as though he understood. I needn't have worried.

Tim has Cerebral Palsy. It took time to gain each other's trust, there were often times when we nearly backed away. I was so cautious. I didn't want to get hurt. Tim was patient, and as time passed, I learnt to trust him.

We had holidays together. It was so nice to be on holiday as a couple. I had looked at other couples together on holiday, and now *we* were a couple on holiday. We have been to Elait, Tenerife, Majorca, Turkey, Italy, Mexico, America and Kenya.

In Kenya we stayed in a beach hotel for 10 days, and then flew in a small plane past Mount Kilimanjaro to a camp in the Masai Mara safari area. I had booked a safari trip for just the two of us with a small company who were willing to help us. We camped in an isolated spot with just eight tents. Our organiser had made minor adjustments to make our tent accessible. He had built a wooden ramp up to the en-suite toilet and fixed a wooden handrail. He had also fixed wooden planks across the dug-out shower area and strapped a simple chair to the planks for me to use for showering. Just the job.

Tim isn't a very good passenger, and cannot cope with bumpy roads; it makes him feel ill. This had been a worry.

Just as we thought, within a few minutes Tim started to feel unwell and we had to stop. Was this going to be a disaster on the first day! The driver asked Tim if he ever experienced this when he drove at home. Tim said that he was always fine, that the concentration of driving and using the wheel for support stopped him feeling ill. The driver said to Tim then maybe you'd better drive. We were both surprised, and Tim swapped places to drive the 4 x 4 drive jeep.

It was Tim who drove us around the tracks, over grassy plains and down and across rocky streams. He didn't feel ill, and loved the experience. We had a Masai Mara guide with us to point out the wildlife. There were plenty of giraffes and zebras. We saw a leopard who had a kill in a tree. We came across a large herd of elephants crossing an open stretch of ground. We got up really early to spot lions and viewed the rare rhinos who are constantly guarded.

We ended our evenings sipping cocktails out in the bush watching the sunset. We told stories around the campfire, and were shown to our tents by a Masai Mara warrior complete with spear. It'd been an amazing holiday. It could have all gone so wrong but, with the right people, anything and everything is possible.

Tim and I went to Turkey for a week. Once there, we found that none of the trips were accessible for us. The young woman in the hotel shop spoke good English and said her brother had a car and could take us out, so we agreed. We went to a lovely local spot with waterfalls, so quiet and away from the tourist rush. We then asked to spend a day in the mountains. We set off early in the morning, climbing higher and higher, with spectacular scenery. The brother didn't speak English, but it wasn't a problem. We arrived at his grandmother's basic dwelling house, which had really magnificent views. We thought it was nice that he'd brought his grandmother's shopping with him. He slept while we gazed at the surrounding views. It was so peaceful.

There were some advantages in doing our own thing, definitely.

Tim and I still visit each other's homes. You might wonder why we haven't moved in together. My bungalow is so suited for me with wide doors, large rooms and various adaptations. It would be hard to find another place so good. I now have no family, but lots of friends around me. Tim likes the independence of his house, which has been his home for all his life. He also has good friends around him. We can be together and yet have our own space.

We have now been together for 25 years and we are definitely soul-mates. We are there for each other whatever the problem. I'm so lucky that eventually I found love with such a lovely man.

CHAPTER 50

TIM

Tim lives in Exmouth. He is the eldest of two brothers. Tim was born with Cerebral Palsy which affects all his limbs and speech. Despite this, Tim learnt to walk with difficulty, ride a bike, and join in all the activities of family life. In fact, his parents never told Tim that he had Cerebral Palsy. Later, they said they did it to protect him. In the 1950s, having a disability was still a stigma and there was a tendency for any disabled child to be sent away to a special school. He attended mainstream schools but found it difficult to keep up with the other children.

Tim's mother became blind as a teenager and could never see her children. His father was a milkman. Tim's maternal grandmother lived with them and helped bring up the two boys. Tim's uncle also lived with them, so it was a family of six.

Tim found that he couldn't do everything his younger brother could do. He found running very difficult, and couldn't do fiddly things like do-up the buttons of his shirt, tie his shoe laces or put on a tie. He thought he was just clumsy, he didn't know any different. Tim struggled at school, finding it difficult to read and write, but loved mathematics. There was no support for any child who was struggling at school in those days, and no-one knew of Tim's disability, not even Tim. He became interested in science later in life but his reading and writing set him back. He struggled with sport at school, just getting ready for sport took a long time.

When he became seven years old, his parents said that he needed to help with the milk round. Tim had to get up at 4.30 a.m. and stand at the end of the road where the milk depot was, to wait for his father. His father knew it was against the law, and never let Tim near the depot. He picked up Tim, who then had to go from door to door delivering milk bottles. On Saturday mornings, Tim was given the receipts to sort out. His mother sent Tim to help his father deliver on several Christmas Days (a time when there were still milk deliveries that day). His younger brother was never asked to help.

Tim continued to struggle with schoolwork, but outside of school, he happily cycled along the beach road with his friends on his bike. He left school with a maths qualification only. His first job was a car panel beater in a garage. After having a medical for work, he was told by his boss he had to leave. At the medical assessment, he learned that he had Cerebral Palsy, which he'd never heard of. No-one explained what Cerebral Palsy was and why he was experiencing so much difficulty in everyday life. He was unemployed for nine months and was then assessed by a Disabled Employment Officer. He was able to get Tim a place at St Lloyd's College in Exeter, which is a college for disabled people. Tim spent two years there, where he did a course in light precision engineering. Tim has poor hand-dexterity but found that he could operate machinery with modified handles and levers. He loved the course and enjoyed the social activities, including trying local pubs with other college friends.

Tim acquired a job at an engineering firm in Exmouth and worked for them in the tool room using a lathe and a milling machine. He was now a fully-skilled engineer after leaving college, but because of his disability, he never received a fully-skilled rate of pay.

After working there for around 25 years full-time, he found that it became too physically demanding to do a full day's work, so went part-time. His grandmother and uncle had died and both parents were older and needing help. When I first got to know Tim, he was working full-time and dashing home during his lunch break to help his parents get their mid-day meal. Within a few years, both parents had died.

Tim was experiencing a lot of pain with swelling joints and weak spells which tired him out. After investigation at the hospital, Tim was told that he had Ankylosing Spondylitis. There was no cure but they said Tim needed to exercise as much as possible to keep the joints flexible – the one thing he found difficult to do. After 10 years, he was told that he probably didn't have the condition.

It came as a big shock. Tim was referred to the hospital for another investigation, and was told that he had Fibromyalgia. This diagnosis exactly matched his conditions of fatigue, weak spells and pain. After working for 32 years, Tim was made redundant. He then had to see a Disability Employment Officer who would suggest other work. The DEO suggested that, once Tom had 'recovered', he could find part-time work for him – somewhere. Tim's doctor said 'No, Tim isn't up to working anymore', and sent a letter confirming this so that Tim was able to retire.

So, Tim retired.

I was admitted to the new unit of our local hospital a while ago, staying in a single room with an accessible bathroom. There was no television but I did have my ipad, and often skyped Tim. On Sunday evening, Tim asked if I was watching the Antiques Roadshow programme. I replied that I couldn't. He sat on the settee at home in Exmouth and put his ipad on the settee beside him, the ipad facing the television screen, so in a way I was sitting beside him watching the show. A nurse came in at that moment and said 'Hi!' and Tim replied 'Hi!' She looked startled; maybe she thought I'd suddenly acquired a deep voice. It was a surreal moment.

While at the hospital, a young nurse came to take my blood pressure and remarked on my suntanned arm. I said that I had not long been back from a holiday in Tenerife with my boyfriend. She said 'You old floozy!' It made me laugh. I never considered myself to be a floozy – a reputation to live up to perhaps!

Now retired, Tim can go at his pace and rest whenever he needs. With help, Tim keeps his house and garden maintained, adding improvements over the years.

Because of his Cerebral Palsy, Tim finds it difficult to read and write, but over time he has found audio formats of books, magazines and newspapers, a great source of information which hadn't been available to him before. He loves researching, especially if it's related to science, weather, climate and the environment; and the history of his hometown Exmouth. And the list continues. He's interested in all kinds of topics.

We're both so glad that we found one another.

CHAPTER 51

A BACK OPERATION

I was getting a lot of backache, even though I wore my spinal brace all day. I had worn a leather back support most of my life; without the brace I could only sit up for a short time. I made an appointment to see a consultant to discuss this. He advised me that I needed an operation to insert a steel rod in my spine to support my back.

First, I had an operation to remove a rib bone, which could then be used along with the steel rod to support my back. I woke to find myself in Intensive Care, having to be turned every fifteen minutes to help my lungs work. After a few days, I returned to the ward. I stayed in hospital for about a week recovering from that operation before the big back operation.

For both operations, I was heavily sedated, where I retreated into a nightmare world. I couldn't explain why I thought the things I imagined were real. When I woke in the ward, most of the beds were empty. It was Easter weekend so most people had gone home. I was convinced that everyone had died, and I was next! In my drugged state of mind, I saw nurses carry dead people around and hide them in cupboards. I tried to tell people but they didn't believe me. Well, of course it wasn't true, it was my weird nightmare, but it has stayed as clear now as when I dreamt it. When my parents visited, I told them they had to sit down, otherwise they'd be gassed. It was an awful place to be. I was so glad when I didn't need the drugs anymore. Apparently, I tried to hit a nurse over the head with a bottle in my desperation to stay alive. I have no recollection of this at all.

I had to stay on my back for everything for the next few weeks. Then they made a padded plastic mould to fit around my back and front, from the tops of my shoulders down to my buttocks. Making sure I was well strapped up, I was able to sit up. After staying in hospital for six weeks, I returned home wearing the mould. I had to wear it day and night for nine months. Carers came in the mornings to roll me out and wash me and then roll me back into the mould again. It was a difficult nine months but I still went back to work.

It was such a good feeling when at last the plaster came off and I could sit up without any support. Now I didn't need to wear a spinal brace or callipers. I had spent nearly fifty years trussed-up and supported with metal bars in order to move. How much my life had changed in the last few years!

A year later, I somehow managed to fracture the steel rod, which dug into me and caused me pain. Within a few days, I was in hospital again. I needed to go through the operation all over again. Another steel rod was inserted and I had to go through another nine months of being encased in a plaster mould.

Having to work and cope with the operations was a struggle. Maybe I didn't need to work, there was only me to think about and support. I'd started work in 1971 when I was 21, and I decided to give up work on ill health grounds in 2001 when I was 52. I'd worked for 30 years, mostly full-time and then part-time. I think I had given it my best shot. Maybe I could go at my own pace now.

It felt weird not having to wear a spinal brace or callipers. They had caused friction on my skin for so long, creating sores and digging into me. I'd longed to be able to sit up in my wheelchair without having to wear any supports. *Now it had become true.* My parents told me that I'd been offered a spine operation when I was twelve, but because the consultant said it might affect my walking, they'd turned it down. I hadn't known this at the time. No-one knows whether or not they've made the right decision, they have to hope that they have. I just knew that I'd now made the right decision for my future.

Life became so much easier for me. I didn't have to watch where I walked in case I slipped and fell. I didn't have to avoid other people in case they knocked me over. Lowered kerbs, level entrances and automatic doors around the town meant that I could get to most places. I loved looking at clothes which didn't have to be altered in any way. I could still be mobile in my adapted van.

My life soon became full. I could have more holidays, go out with friends. I love the outdoors, the countryside and the sea. Friends joined me to explore the area. I was always on the look-out for accessible walks, and this continues; I'm always looking for more places to go.

One of the things I had always wished I could do was to walk by the seashore close to the waves. I thought it must be the most wonderful feeling. The sand is usually too soft for my wheelchair and I generally watched from a distance. Izzy was always determined to try and get me to the water's edge whenever possible. One time when we were visiting Sidmouth, Izzy carried a beach chair down to the water's edge and then asked two burly men if they could lift me down so that I could feel the waves on my feet. It was delicious. I could paddle my feet.

Another time, some friends and I went to Sidmouth and saw a really high tide covering a concrete slipway. Andrea, Eileen and Sarah all joined me and my wheelchair for a paddle on the concrete slipway, laughing as the waves rolled in. I have always looked out for this to happen again, but it never has, which made that day very special and memorable.

When on holiday, my friends sometimes dragged the wheelchair to the water's edge so that I could dangle my feet in the sea. Never very good for the wheelchair, I know, but what was important – me or the wheelchair? Rachael and I went to Barcelona for a few days and we caught a train to the coast for the day. I watched as Rachael went for a paddle along the shoreline. She came back with a plastic bag full of seawater so that I could have a paddle. It was so nice that she made sure I wasn't left out of our seaside experience.

CHAPTER 52

SAILING OVERSEAS

Ann and I had the opportunity to become crew on the *Lord Nelson* and sail around the Bahamas.

The *Lord Nelson,* owned by the Jubilee Sailing Trust, is a specially-designed three-mast square rigger, with full access for able and disabled crew members, to take a full part in running the ship. We flew to mainland Bahamas, and another small plane took us to Grand Bahamas Island. We were greeted by a hot sun and swaying palm trees in the gentle breeze.

We wandered around the local markets, amazed at the variety of food and crafts. Everyone was so friendly. One lady slapped the back of my wheelchair as I wheeled along and said 'Rock on, man!' which made us all laugh. We sipped cocktail drinks with exotic flavours and chose straw hats to keep off the sun. As we admired a Hibiscus flower, a humming bird came to feed, and showed off its magnificent feathers.

We boarded the *Lord Nelson* and signed on as crew. We met the rest of the crew who were from England, America, Ecuador and the Bahamas.

The day dawned bright and clear as we headed for the open seas. Working as a team, we soon had all the sails up, and they shone in the blue sky as we rolled along.

We dropped anchor near a remote island near the Berry Islands; I could see the golden white sands and emerald green sea with palm trees along the shore. We had a chance to go snorkelling. I was hoisted down to the waiting dinghy, and sat on the edge of the dinghy, holding onto the others as we headed towards a rocky area. We had our snorkelling gear on. We were told, when the dinghy stops, to fall backwards into the sea. Before I had a chance to worry about this, I went back with the others and hit the water.

I looked around me and gasped; I had entered another world. As the sun's rays hit the water, everything seemed to sparkle. A large shoal of turquoise-striped fish swam in unison. There were so many different types of colourful coral with small creatures and fish darting around. I was spellbound by the beauty of it all.

We swam to the shore to join the other crew who had reached the beach for a barbeque. In the afternoon we had another chance to swim out for a while before boarding the dinghy and heading back to the *Lord Nelson*. By sunset, we had left our tropical island and sailed into the night.

I was on early watch and saw the world gently coming alive. As the sun rose, the sky turned to amber and yellow before becoming bright blue for another hot day. We sailed into Nassau Harbour and after a Happy Hour of cleaning the ship, we went ashore to explore the island and sample the local food.

It was all hands to the braces as we pulled on the sails and spanker, allowing the wind to push us away from Nassau harbour and back toward Berry Islands for our return trip. By now, we were like one big family, knowing everyone's name and learning about each other's cultures.

Working on the sails, watch duty plus our time helping in the kitchen, kept us all busy. One afternoon I had the chance to be hoisted aloft as we sailed along. It was exhilarating to be winched up among the sails with only the blue sea surrounding us. At night while on watch I was amazed at the starlit sky, so many stars shining back at us. At midnight it was still so warm as we sailed into the dark. Just our ship moving along with the waves and the gentle wind. We approached our remote island and dropped anchor for the night.

We went snorkelling again the next morning, but I noticed large groups of small jellyfish and I kept being stung. As I headed for the shore, I spotted a stingray. After a quick picnic on shore, we had to head back to the ship as a storm was approaching. We later learnt from local people that jellyfish near the shore means stormy weather approaching. We had to rely on the weather station.

We dressed in our oilskins as we worked in soft, warm rain. It seemed just as nice to be outside. The wind rose to force six and the ship sprang alive as she bounced through the waves, which sprayed over the decks, and the wind bellowed through the sails. By the morning, the storm had passed and we were back to the gentle roll of the ship as we headed towards the end of our trip.

A few years later, I flew out to the Canary Islands with some friends to join the *Lord Nelson* and sail around the islands. We left the harbour of Puerto Rico and headed for Fuerteventura with a strong wind behind us. We sailed through the night.

The next morning we spotted a remote sandy beach which looked idyllic; we dropped anchor and went by dinghies to the shore for a picnic. We had landed on a German nudist beach! It didn't take long before we were surrounded by naked people, all wanting to know about us. It certainly was an interesting experience.

We headed back to Tenerife and dropped anchor by some cliffs and a shingle beach. I lay in my bunk and listened to the waves on the shingle as I drifted into sleep. In the morning we piled into taxis and headed up to the volcano, Mount Teide. With the snow around us, we could look down and see our ship in the distance. I was always very proud of her when I could see her from ashore.

We set sail for Gomera. While eating on the deck, a pod of dolphins swam beside the ship. It was lovely to see them arc out of the water as we sailed along.

I was on the midnight watch. As I reported for duty, we were rolling gently along with virtually no wind. At around 3.00 a.m., I took my position at the helm for a while. Suddenly, a strong wind hit the ship, the sails filled and we were off gaining speed in the water. It was an amazing experience to feel the power of the wind. After a while the captain was concerned that if we continued to move at this new speed, we would completely miss the island of Gomera. We needed to slow down by taking down some sails.

With most of the crew asleep, the captain asked if I was alright to stay at the helm while he helped the rest of the watch lower the sails. I was tired, but exhilarated at being given the responsibility of helming by myself in the dark. I glued my eyes to the compass to keep the wheel in the right position, to be sure to go the right way. I think they had to prise me out of the seat in the end, I was so tired and stiff, but to this day, I have never forgotten the experience.

We hired four-wheeled drive vehicles and drove up the steep tree-covered mountains and explored inland. So different from the other Canary Islands. The local people shout or sing to communicate with each other, with winches across the ravines for transport. We saw homes perched on the edge of high places.

Ann and I booked to sail around the Caribbean on Tenacious, the new wooden-built ship. We left Antigua and sailed to Dominica. Once there, we were lifted into long rowing boats and the local people used the paddles as we silently moved along the narrow river through remote jungle landscape. It felt eerie as some trees formed a canopy over us and had weird shapes. No-one spoke, I think we were all awed by the experience. We stopped at a remote bar for the legendary drink Dynamite Punch.

We set sail for a small French-owned island, Iles des Saintes, where Euros is the currency. It seemed strange to be so far from home and using Euros; we had come from the sparsely populated island of Dominica to a modern island, full of fashion shops and designer jewellery. We found a lovely sandy beach for a swim before setting sail again. Our next destination was Pigeon Island, halfway up the west coast of Guadeloupe. Bad weather stopped us from going ashore, but we had already experienced so much.

Ann and I flew to Boston to join Tenacious for a Tall Ship Festival near New York, along with many other Tall Ships from around the world. We arrived a few days early to explore Boston. We ordered a wheelchair-accessible taxi, hoping we could travel in one taxi to keep the price down. Ann needed to get in the back, my wheelchair could only go folded-up in the back with her. I could put a little bit of weight on one leg, but the passenger seat was far too high for me to transfer, and I said to the driver 'If I stand up and turn round, can you reach across the driver's seat, grab my trousers, and yank me in?' It worked, with me grabbing rails to try and help. From then on every time we needed a taxi, I asked them to grab my trousers and pull. I was really hoping that the trousers didn't split and was, luckily, spared that embarrassment.

It was very foggy for the festival, and whenever we sailed, we had to constantly use the fog horn. In fact, we took part in a Tall Ship Parade and I wondered how anyone could actually see us. We spent a lot of time showing people around while in dock.

I went with Ann and some friends to a local restaurant. On our return, we were apprehended by the police. We had no identity with us, and were escorted to the local police station for some hours until they received evidence that we should be on Tenacious. Did we really look like dodgy people?

My last sailing trip was in 2005. I was finding it harder to cope. Night watches drained my energy and I found transferring difficult on solid ground, let alone a moving ship. It was with reluctance that I made the decision to stop sailing, but nothing can take away the wonderful and exciting experiences and the friendships I have made over many years.

CHAPTER 53

To Australia and Beyond

I wanted to explore Australia, and my friend Izzy came with me. We decided on a ten-week trip and I spent months planning the trip, making sure everything would be accessible. In September 2002 with me pulling my bag on wheels, Izzy with her haversack, we boarded the plane for Singapore, staying for a few nights to explore the culture and city life.

We then started our Australian journey in Perth. It was cold after Singapore. The city is compact, and after a few days we caught a small plane northwards to Monkey Mia – a remote spot by the sea with just scrubland around us. We stayed at a centre where local dolphins are encouraged to come to the shore daily for fish. The dolphins are wild and so it's their decision whether they come or not, but as dolphins are very inquisitive and eager for free food, they are likely to appear. The water was so inviting that Izzy ran down to the seashore and paddled her feet.

She returned saying that she must have hit her toe on something, it hurt. Later we heard how to shuffle into the sea so as not to disturb small stingray. That is obviously what

Izzy had done, not a good start. I got into the accessible beach buggy which took me into the sea to feed the dolphins. They came really close and took fish from our hands as the warden explained about the dolphins' life.

We flew to Ayres Rock, or Uluru – its now preferred name, in the Uluru-Kata Tjuta National Park. We hired a car and drove to the only wheelchair-accessible hotel, which was also the most expensive hotel. We bought food supplies from the supermarket.

We followed the signposts to see the famous big red rock in the middle of the desert. We couldn't see it, so how far away were we? We looked around us. Suddenly we drove around a corner and nearly hit it, it was that close. It suddenly loomed up in front of us. We just went *Wow!* The hotel complex was sunk into the ground, so we'd had to drive up to the right level. We were spellbound by the majestic way it emerged from the surrounding bush land.

We parked in the sunset viewing area and joined others to watch the colours of the rock change as the sun set. Everyone was whispering, it felt as though we were intruding in this magical nature show. The next morning we rose before sunrise, wrapped up, and faced the freezing weather to drive in the semi- darkness to the other side of the rock to see the sun rise. The rock seemed so different from this side and the colours equally spectacular. We joined the warden for a free guide around the area and saw aborigine artwork. We then drove to see the Olgas, a set of impressive domes of a similar age. We stopped to eat some cheese sandwiches for lunch, but it was so hot, the cheese had completely melted.

We flew to Darwin and the humidity added to the heat. I had already booked two road trips but hadn't appreciated just how long they were. We did a day trip to the Kakado National Park and travelled 600 miles in one day. The aborigine paintings were stunning. I baked in the heat as a boat trip took us along a remote river amongst the crocodiles and spectacular birdlife. The following day we did a half-day trip to the Lichfield National Park, which again was a 400 mile round-trip. We were taken to a lovely pool of water in the middle of the jungle with a spectacular waterfall. The guide said we could have a swim, and assured us there were no crocodiles. We quickly changed, and scrambled over the rocks to the water; all thought of what might be lurking around us forgotten.

At Cairns, we picked up our hire car for the week. I had booked a log cabin in the hills. It was a lot more remote than we thought, and the facilities were basic. I had a shower with bore hole water and came out smelling worse. We were plagued with insects and geckos. We pulled the double bed into the middle of the room, away from the creepy insects, but still tossed and turned thinking they were in bed with us. A pillow fell to the floor and neither of us wanted to pick the pillow up, so we shared a pillow. Maybe we weren't such country people after all! We left the next day.

We had no map of the area and drove until we saw signs to the coast road. By evening, we had reached Port Douglas on the coast. The first big hotel had a wheelchair-accessible room for one night, and we collapsed into bed. Fortunately, they re-arranged bookings, and we stayed. We loved Port Douglas. It was small and laid back. We strolled around a market and joked with the locals. We paddled in the warm sea, complete with my wheelchair.

We went by boat to the Barrier Reef and there was a special seat which wound down to the ocean so that I could also snorkel. The waves were a bit rough and Izzy wasn't sure, but with life jackets we were fine. We'd covered ourselves in sun protection lotion, but Izzy hadn't done the backs of her legs, and as the life jacket took her higher out of the water, she had sunburn – and she then found it hard to sit down for several days after.

We joined the famous scenic railway as it wound its way up into the rainforest to Kuranda. There was a specific space for a wheelchair, so I didn't miss out on anything. There was a running commentary about the area and what to look out for. We returned downhill in a cable car as we flew over the rainforest. We stopped on the way down on a wooden walkway and wandered around to learn more about them.

We stayed in a backpackers hostel at Hervey Bay to go whale watching, an amazing experience. I had the chance to join a trip to Fraser Island. There are no roads, but four-wheel drive vehicles drove easily over the sandy landscape. They agreed to take me, but no wheelchair. Once we reached it by ferry, I was lifted into the vehicle and seated, and we explored the island. For lunch, I was carried into the dining room and was seated in an ordinary chair to join the others. It kind of worked. Later, the 4WD returned along the long sandy shore, with wind flowing through our hair. It was exhilarating.

We arrived in Sydney by train and stayed in the local YMCA. We did all the sights. We took a ferry to Manley to see the coastline. We spent a day exploring the Blue Mountains and watched kangaroos grazing as dusk came.

After a fourteen-hour train ride, we arrived in Melbourne.

We visited the Great Ocean Road to see the twelve apostles: a collection of limestone rocks off the shore of the

Port Campbell National Park. We travelled to Phillip Island to see the small fairy penguins come home at dusk to feed their young.

We had to fly from Melbourne to New Zealand via a stop in Sidney; one of our least impressive experiences. At Melbourne, they booked our luggage and my wheelchair to be taken directly to the flight to New Zealand. I didn't realise how this would affect me until I reached Sidney: no wheelchair. They supplied an airport wheelchair. Then I was told we had landed in the local airport and had to go by coach to the international airport. We reached the coach, which was not accessible for me, and no-one was either willing or able to get me onboard. As the minutes ticked by, Izzy heaved me up the steps to a seat; the wheelchair couldn't come with us. At the international airport, again, no-one was willing to help. Izzy went off to try and find an airport wheelchair and then heaved me down into it. The driver complained that he was going to be late. We were late too! We could hear our names on the Tannoy system. We were rushed through while the flight staff complained that we were late. We had no time to explain.

We left Australia and flew to New Zealand. We picked up our hire car in Christchurch, complete with acceleration and brake adaptations for me, and after a night in the YMCA we headed down to the Fjordland. As we drove to Milford Sound it poured with rain. We emerged from the high Homer Tunnel pass to see snow; we had about 3 ft of snow and ice both sides of us.

The boat trip and waterfalls were spectacular because of the rain. We quickly drove away from the area before the mountain pass gates closed for the night. After a while, we swapped seats for me to drive. Inquisitive Kia parrots had landed on the roof of our car and pecked at Izzy's head every time she tried to get out of the car. A warden told us to hurry up, as there had been an avalanche warning, and he followed us all the way out of the danger area.

We drove to Queenstown and along the snow- peaked mountain region. The west coast area was covered in a thick wooded area with tree ferns. At Franz Joseph we had a helicopter flight over the two glaciers. I stayed in the helicopter while Izzy and two other girls had a short walk around. I asked if I could have a glacier experience certificate too; apparently not, as I hadn't walked on the glacier. Then we left the South Island and caught the ferry to the North Island.

We explored the thermal area of Rotaroua and used the warm thermal pool at the Youth Hostel. We drove up the highway to the scenic Bay of Islands. It was on this highway I got stopped by the police for speeding. I never, ever speed; Izzy often complained about how slow I went. I had sped-up to overtake some slow lorries in the middle lane; that was enough to alert the police, who pulled me over and asked to see my licence. Once he realised that we had only three days left in New Zealand, he let us go.

Izzy swam with the dolphins while I went for a boat trip around the islands. We wanted to look at the Treaty House and Culture Centre about four miles away, but there were no local accessible taxis. Izzy spotted a small Asian tuk-tuk parked by the taxi rank. We might not have thought it possible, but knowing we had used them in Sri Lanka, we soon persuaded the driver that we could get on board with a folded wheelchair and reach the area.

All was well.

The only way back was to walk along a path by the sea. It was warm as we strolled along in the peace and quiet. We walked side by side holding hands and chatting. It was so flat, Izzy's arm was easily pulling me along in my wheelchair. We drove back down to Auckland along the west coast and stopped at a completely deserted beach for our lunch along the way. We spent a few nights in the Sky City Hotel, complete with Sky Tower and a casino. We did try a few flutters, won and lost, but not much. Our money was precious.

We flew onto Fiji and had a 2-hour drive to our hotel on the south coast. It was hot as we drove past sugarcane fields and palm trees. Everyone was saying 'Bula!' – their local greeting. We joined a local village and watched as they prepared a traditional earth-oven meal, and we were entertained by local dances and singing. The Fijian people were so friendly, sincere and yet quietly spoken and calming.

We had a few days to take it easy. I was tired and relaxed in the shade while Izzy laid on the sun bed and then went canoeing around the rock pools. She was very quiet that evening and I discovered why the following day; she was so sunburnt she could hardly move. I pointed out that I had seen her with a bottle of sun protection cream, but she replied that, because of the light cloud cover, she hadn't bothered to put any on. I got a breakfast tray and left it by her bed. Slowly, as the day progressed, the food disappeared. I was worried because we were flying to Los Angeles the next day. How she got up and did the journey I do not know, but she did. We crossed the 'date line' and arrived in Los Angeles before we had departed. All very confusing.

In contrast, we arrived in the hustle and bustle of Los Angeles and queued for a taxi get to our hotel in the Hollywood area. We strolled along the Hall of Fame and explored Hollywood. We needed to catch the train to San Francisco, but the train was late due to the lack of a buffet coach. We sat on the platform for hours, and by then we were very tired. Ten weeks of constant travelling was getting to us as we propped each other up at the station.

The train arrived and there was a whole coach for disabled people or 'handicapped' as it's known in America. Some people had sleeping bags to sleep in. The train was travelling the whole length of America over about three days. (Our trip was 24 hours but we got off and stayed at a hotel for the night.) People complained about the train being late. After a couple of complaints, there was an announcement by the buffet staff to only come if you had a smile. There was another announcement for English cream teas being served, and another for a film show.

Apparently, there is no train station in the centre of San Francisco. Everyone has to board coaches and be driven into the centre, which took about an hour. The coaches are meant to be accessible, but the lift was broken, so I was lifted up the steps in my wheelchair.

It was near midnight when we arrived. It looked dark and spooky as we tried to find a taxi to our hotel. Everyone had disappeared so quickly. The coach driver very kindly stopped a taxi and persuaded him to take us. Maybe not as simple as we'd thought.

San Francisco is so hilly, we took a taxi to experience the steep slopes often used in films. Izzy explored Alcatraz, while I explored Pier 39 and watched the sea lions basking in the sun. Before we knew it, the ten weeks were up, and we had to squash everything we had bought into our cases and return home. We felt as though we had conquered the world.

Izzy had been on so many trips with me and we always had fun together. She was determined that I should take part in everything and be an equal. When the taxi took us from Melbourne to the airport, the driver charged an exorbitant amount for carrying the wheelchair and Izzy argued with him all the way to the airport. I had to drag her away in order to catch the plane. 'It's not right!' she said.

CHAPTER 54

AFRICA

I have been to Africa quite a few times and love the people, the scenery and the animals. It is absolutely magical.

Many years ago, I had the opportunity to visit Zimbabwe for a holiday and stayed at the Victoria Springs Hotel, a luxury hotel but affordable with the package deal. Pauline (the second Pauline I've had as a good friend) and I flew with Air Namibia to Zimbabwe, via Namibia and Zambia, which made the flight cheaper.

The airport in Namibia was in the middle of nowhere. We boarded coaches to spend a few hours in Windhoek, the Capital. We arrived in Zambia during an evening thunderstorm and I had to be man-handled down the steps to my wheelchair. We rushed to the border of Zambia before the border closed at 8.00 p.m. and so reach our destination of Victoria Falls.

Our first visit was, of course, to the magnificent Victoria Falls. We followed the pathway through the rainforest along the top of the gorge, with monkeys playing around us. The further we went, the wetter we became as the spray filled the air. The noise was deafening as tons of water flowed over the edge along the gorge. We were virtually on our own, no real sign of tourism apart from a local man selling waterproof ponchos at the gate. Victoria Falls is known to the locals as *The River That Thunders* which is very apt. At the furthest point, there was a constant rainbow. It was hard to drag ourselves away. We also flew over the falls in a helicopter to see just how long the gorge and waterfalls are. We saw rainbow after rainbow.

We left early for our trip to Botswana. We stopped at Mowana Lodge by the river. We boarded safari vehicles and drove off in search of wildlife. We didn't have far to go, the whole area was teaming with a wide variety of wildlife. There were elephants, impala, waterbuck, puku, zebra, warthogs and lots more. On a boat trip we viewed hippos. On our way back to the hotel we had to stop near the hotel to let a herd of elephants wander by.

We decided to walk across the boundary bridge between Zimbabwe and Zambia to view the waterfalls from the other side. We queued at the tiny customs building to have our passports stamped as we were leaving Zimbabwe. We had to walk around local women busy washing by the outside tap. While being squashed into the hut waiting to show our passports, I realised Pauline's passport was missing. I tried not to panic, but it was *not* a place to lose a passport. One local chap kept tapping my arm. I tried to ignore him as I searched for the passport. Then he said 'You've dropped a passport!' and there it was on the floor. What a relief!

The actual bridge seemed to be in no-man's land and was about a mile long. We made our way across the bridge in the heat of the sun to Zambia and queued in their customs building.

We explored the local area and viewed the waterfall from the other side. Once off the bridge and back in Zimbabwe again, we fell into a shabby taxi for the hotel. We had forgotten to ask how much the fare would be; it turned out to be the equivalent of 50p.

There was an impressive old tree that people talked about just outside of town, so we went to see it by taxi, and decided to walk back to the hotel. The taxi driver was reluctant to leave us there, but we said 'We're fine', and he disappeared. The way back was much longer than we realised, and more perilous than we imagined.

The path was good and we set off in high spirits, trying to dodge elephant dung. Not sure what we would do if a herd of elephants came along, but we continued. We sat by the edge of the Zambezi river, dipping our feet in the water to cool ourselves. Then we saw a dilapidated wooden sign saying 'Beware of Crocodiles' and so we quickly moved on. The path went on forever and we got hotter with the sun beating down on us. We stopped to watch the monkeys in the trees.

Eventually, we collapsed into the shade of the hotel lobby. One of the receptionists asked where we had been, so we explained that we had walked from the famous tree. She said that there is a particularly large nasty crocodile living in that area which had killed nine people so far that year! Also, there were outlaws in the jungle who could have mugged us. We'd taken a huge risk without knowing it.

We explored a traditional African village and chatted to local people. Both Pauline and I had our fortunes told by a witchdoctor, who told me I would live until I was at least 70.

We enjoyed a Sundowners trip on the Zambezi River.

Izzy, Gina and I flew to Johannesburg and joined a company who specialises in safaris for disabled people around the Kalahari Wildlife Reserve. The organisers had adapted a large vehicle with a lift at one side up to a viewing area with open sides. We trundled along the road with the wind in our hair heading to the park. We stayed in organised, protected accommodation within the park, but the organisers did all their own cooking with everything stored in the van.

We left early every morning to view the animals feeding at sunrise, and then returned for breakfast. We travelled from one area to another staying in different accommodation, from a woven hut, to a tent. We tried to cope in our tent with torches in the dark only to learn there was electricity on a pole inside the tent. It never occurred to me. Why didn't they tell us?

The roads in the reserve were quite busy, it was difficult for the large vehicle to find quieter routes. If another vehicle stopped, it was usually because they had spotted something, so everyone stopped. One morning I was desperate for the toilet. The driver agreed to pull in while I discreetly used the emergency bedpan. That was fine but everyone else also stopped their cars to see what we had spotted. I groaned as more cars pulled up.

After the safari, we stayed in Cape Town for a few days. We travelled up by lift to visit Tabletop Mountain. We had to choose a day when the clouds stayed clear. The view was spectacular. We watched protected penguins from an overhead boardwalk and drove down to the Cape of Good Hope.

We spent the last afternoon shopping at the harbour and enjoyed the local cider. We were a bit tipsy as we wandered back to the hotel. The front wheel of my wheelchair hit a rut while crossing a bridge and all the gifts on my lap raised off and started falling over the bridge into the harbour. Our reactions were slow as we tried to grab them. We stared in disbelief at our lost gifts floating, and sinking, but then we found it funny – blame it on the cider. At least *we* were fine.

Lynn and I flew to the east coast of Africa and made our way to St Lucia, a picturesque village situated within a nature reserve and near the coast. I wanted to go whale-watching. We travelled along the beach to a small boat by the shoreline. I was transferred from my wheelchair to an old shower chair, then I was hauled from the van to the boat across a plank of wood. Then I transferred to the bench on the boat.

My feet didn't touch the floor, and people hung to each side of me while a tractor pushed us into the waves with a long pole. The waves tossed us everywhere. I saw an extremely large wave heading straight for us; it would have definitely swamped the boat. The captain turned the boat sidewards, and drove the boat expertly along the base of the large wave, at high speed. My heart was in my mouth as I looked up at the wave. Seated sideways, I was looking straight at it. I looked behind us and saw the wave collapsing. Were we going to make it? The end of the wave came and we slowed down.

What a relief!

I felt drained just experiencing that.

We spent two hours following a whale and calf, but rarely saw them. We did see dolphins swimming with the boat. We used a similar huge wave to get us back to shore again. Just getting out to sea had got my adrenaline going.

On another trip, I was lifted onto a river boat to see hippos and other wildlife. We visited the ancient World Heritage Site at False Bay and walked along a wooden boardwalk to the coast along the river. There was just us, and trees, and the warm breeze with hippos snoozing.

We stayed at a Game Reserve. The wildlife freely walked around the lodges, where Impala deer and warthog grazed alongside. We found that if we were quiet, we could creep onto our patio and watch the wildlife around us. There was a beautiful accessible lounge and timber deck overlooking a lake where we could watch the incredible birdlife and the African sunset.

We also explored the Umfolozi Hluhluwe Game Reserve, home of black and white rhino.

My last trip to Africa was a camping safari trip with a friend, Helen. We flew to Johannesburg and then on to a small airport at Maun close to the Okavango Delta Game reserve in Botswana. A volcano had erupted in Iceland just before our trip and many flights were cancelled. Luckily, the all-clear was given just before our trip.

We drove north for several miles and across sandy tracks to stay at a lodge for a few days. I really wanted to meet the Kalahari bushmen in their surroundings. Most of the trips into the bush are done on foot, but because the sand was too soft for my wheelchair, I went on the back of a truck, and we followed the bush people. They explained their culture and how they found food. They lit a fire and cooked us samples of the food they ate. I was amazed how they could find food and water in such a barren land.

In the evening, we sat around a campfire and heard lions roaring. There was a lion enclosure nearby. They had been rescued, as they were causing trouble to nearby villages. The owner was trying to change their eating habits so they would only go for wild game. He was putting something in the cattle meat so that the lions didn't want to eat it. We were able to enter the enclosure on the back of a truck.

We had one spare day at the lodge after the other visitors had left. The bushmen we'd watched were protected by the lodge, but there were other bush people way out in the bush unprotected. With one of the family from the lodge, we headed into the wilderness on the back of the truck. After a couple of hours we stopped in a large area of bush land. Gradually, the bush people appeared, greeting the lady who was with us. I was lifted out of the truck and into the shade. The group consisted of about 15 adults with probably as many children.

They were as interested in me in my wheelchair as I was in them. They made jewellery out of ostrich shell which they wanted me to buy. The lady said that the lodge was full of jewellery they had bought, to help the bush people get supplies they couldn't find in the bush. Their main problem was finding enough water and food, as they had lost their rights to hunt. One elderly lady said, 'If we have to live in the town, we will die.' The bush land was their home.

The local lodges regularly brought out tanks of water to fill up their cans. The children played games and showed us how they practise with a spear, even though they're not allowed to use it. As we left, they shouted out something in their local language. They had said 'Please don't forget us.' I found it very emotional. It seemed a very poignant request. What is happening to our world?

The second part of our trip was to travel into the Okavango Delta and camp within the safari park. It took us all day to reach the area. The reserve had experienced some heavy rains; what had been a small stream was now a fast flowing larger stream which we had to cross. I watched as the vehicle in front of us nearly got washed away and then it was our turn. We followed, holding our breath.

The tents had camp beds and a portable toilet in a separate section, but it was difficult negotiating the sandy soil to move around our floor space.

The next day we boarded the safari vehicle using a side lift to get me to the viewing area for our early morning trip out. Because of the rains we spent the day getting stuck and relying on other vehicles to pull us out, and then having to rescue them. Then our vehicle got stuck again and started sinking sideways. Helen climbed to the outside of the vehicle on the other side to try and rebalance it while our guide found logs to put under the wheel. Very slowly, we managed to free ourselves.

The night was pitch-black as I tried to have a shower in the tent with hot water from the fire and a small torch to see by. I woke in the night to hear lions roaring. This time there were no protective fences to keep them out. It was a strange feeling.

We drove to another area the following day and saw so much wildlife. In a secluded spot we saw a lion and lioness lying beside one another. One of the ladies asked if she could stand up to take a photo – but she stood up too quickly. Within seconds, the lioness went into a crouch position, ready to attack. We froze. The guide told her to sit back down very slowly. After what seemed like an eternity, the lioness moved back to lie beside her mate. We quickly left and realized how vulnerable we could be. The vehicle was open all around which was great for taking photos, but we had to take care.

When I needed the toilet the guide took out a chair with a hole in the middle. He put it behind the truck and let me down in the lift. I disappeared to the back of the truck hoping that no-one was going to find me interesting while there. It actually worked really well and the chair could be folded up afterwards and put away.

The next day we moved to another campsite in the Southern Chobe National Park. We passed a water hole and could see a group of elephants heading our way. We stopped and got our cameras ready. The elephants went straight into the waterhole, drinking and spraying water around, the young trying to join in. After a few minutes, they were gone. The guide explained that they do a certain route nearly every day so that the younger elephants are trained to know what to do. They cover long distances and have to keep going.

The guide kept seeing cheetah paw prints and eventually we glimpsed one creeping along the grass around some zebra.

Every night we were served amazing meals cooked on a small open fire. In the mornings, we had fresh bread made each day in a small bread oven suspended over the fire.

On the last day, we visited a lodge and took a boat trip along the Chobe river. We felt a bit scruffy, having camped for a week. Suddenly – luxury! There was a toilet I could flush, and water coming from a tap, but it didn't really compare to spending an evening around the fire listening to the buzz of the animals in the bush.

As we drove to the airport, we heard that the volcano had erupted again. The wind had changed direction and so, luckily for us, it didn't affect our flights.

The African Continent is alive and vibrant. I was going to miss it – it had been an experience I knew I'd never forget.

CHAPTER 55

South America

Lynn and I flew on Brazilian Airways to San Juan, and changed flight for Peru. We landed in Lima, where we stayed the night.

The next day we caught the plane for Cusco. We had our first glimpse of the towering Andes as we flew higher, with its snow-capped mountains rising into the sky. We landed in bright sunshine and were 3,399 metres high in the mountains. It was difficult to understand the lack of air up there, as everything looked the same. There are little airbags in my wheelchair cushion and they became rock hard. We had also brought some packets of crisps with us, and they looked as though they were about to explode with the lower air pressure.

We were met by our guide, along with his two assistants and the driver. The van was spacious, with separate ramps at the back, and we were driven through Cusco to our hotel.

It was evening by the time we reached our room, and it had become very cold. Temperatures could be as high as 20c during the day but -10c at night, and this was June. The only heating we had was a small portable radiator. It was a case of putting on layers of clothing. Our room was spacious with twin beds. The toilet was quite low but it did have hand rails. One side of our room was built against an old Inca temple. In the Reception, there was an urn of hot water with coca leaves at the side to make tea for anyone with altitude sickness.

Later that evening, we walked along to see a folklore performance. It was freezing, I hadn't realised just how cold it would be in the evenings. The theatre itself was cold and everyone wore layers, making them look twice the size. During the interval we were all offered hot coca leaf tea. Coca leaves are used to make Cocaine. We were always being offered it to drink. The locals chew on the leaves to get a better effect. It's a wonder we weren't going around on a permanent high.

The next morning our guide suggested a boat trip along the Rio Vilcanota river in the Sacred Valley. It was another sunny day as we drove through villages, watching local people working in the fields. It was as if time had stood still.

Eventually we stopped by the river. I looked for a nice little boat to sit on – but there was no boat. Lynn and I looked at each other, and said nothing. Once outside the van, I said 'Where's the boat?' Our guide pointed to a rolled-up dinghy on the top of the van. I gulped; this wasn't what I was expecting.

The boat was pumped up. Our guide gave us life jackets and helmets. I said quietly, 'This isn't going to be a rapid ride, is it?' 'Oh no,' he said, 'just a gentle boat ride.'

I was lifted into the middle section of the boat, and made sure they tied me down to the rubber sausage-looking seat, as I had doubts of being able to stay on, having no balance at all. Lynn, I didn't know until then, couldn't swim, and was scared of water. She looked at me as if to say: *Why didn't you tell me?* but this had come as a surprise to me as well.

Lynn sat beside me and I hung on to her as we pushed away from the shore and started to glide down the river. Two of the men were in the front with paddles and the guide was at the back, also paddling. The sun was out with blue skies and I thought, this is going to be very pleasant. We drifted down the river with the guide pointing out the landscape around us, old Inca settlements and sacred sites. We floated past villages, and children waved to us from the bank of the river. The van had taken my wheelchair downstream.

Then I watched as the water seemed to be running faster and rougher, and saw what I thought was a small rapid ahead. We swished through it at great speed and I hung to Lynn for dear life. I remarked that I hoped *that* would be as exciting as it got. Leo said that everything would be fine, which then made me wonder what was ahead. The river settled down again and all was quiet. We saw heron, a humming bird and other birds by the side of the river.

We passed a few more small rapids and I felt quite brave at being so calm. I was still hanging onto Lynn. Then in the distance, I saw what was in store for us – a larger rapid. I hung on even tighter as Lynn and I looked at each other. Before we knew it, the boat speeded-up and with loud instructions from the guide, everyone paddled fiercely to dodge the rocks either side. We plunged over and around the rocks and then the dinghy got caught on a rock and we were stuck at an angle. I leant heavily against Lynn who was trying to prop me up and stay in the dinghy. We were being soaked by water splashing around us. Suddenly we were free and the dinghy followed the river at great speed.

The river settled down again, and the dinghy was directed to the side of the river, where we saw the van and my wheelchair, which I was very glad to see again. I would never have agreed to a rapid ride, but at the same time we were on a high to think we had achieved this; and survived.

I'd suffered from a headache since I arrived because of the height above sea level and it had become gradually worse. In the end, I agreed to see a doctor, who gave me an injection and some oxygen, and told me to rest for the day. I was suffering from altitude sickness.

I was fine the next day, and we explored the Sacred Valley before arriving in Ollantaytambo for the night. We stopped at a settlement where we were able to feed llamas and alpacas. We watched local people spinning and weaving using wool that had been dyed using local plants. We also stopped at the craft market in Pisac and had a ceramic lesson in Urubamba.

We arrived in Ollantaytambo, a village in the Sacred Valley of Peru, set on the Urubamba River amid snow-capped mountains. The village is an Inca-era grid of cobblestoned streets and small stone-built houses. It took all four men to get my wheelchair over the large cobblestones.

We had the opportunity to enter one of the small stone-built houses; it was just one big room with beds in one corner, a fireplace in the other, a shelf containing charms, and a recess with revered skulls of ancestors. I had to try not to run-over guinea pigs – they were everywhere. The husband threw down some corn and even more guinea pigs emerged from the corners of the room. Guinea pigs are special to the local people and a good source of food. There were plants of every description hanging from the ceiling to dry. On a table nearby there were homemade embroidered textiles which I couldn't resist.

We stayed in a hotel by the station ready for our trip to Machu Picchu the next day. The hotel consisted of little chalets in the grounds.

We had an early night. During the night, I needed to visit the toilet. I don't know how it happened, but one minute I was on the toilet and the next minute I was on the floor. I kept calling Lynn and she padded into the bathroom and asked me what I was doing on the floor. She tried to get me up, but couldn't.

Lynn rang Reception for help. A local man answered, who only knew a few words in English. His answer was either 'More hot water,' or 'More heating.' Then Lynn kept repeating the room number in the hope that he came. It worked, and there was a knock on the door. A Peruvian man appeared, wrapped in layers of ponchos. Lynn pointed to me on the floor and he said 'Oh!' He put his arms under my arms and quickly lifted me back into my wheelchair. He must've had so much strength for a man of relatively short stature. I think that had to be a first for him, and for me as well. We tried to get back to sleep, but it was soon morning.

We caught the early train and swayed along the valley and up towards the nearest station, Machu Picchu Pueblo (also known as Aguas Calientes). Local people were selling their wares along the track. We looked up and saw snow-capped mountains towering over us. I was lifted onto a bus, which wound its way up the steep road to reach Machu Picchu at the top of the mountain.

I caught my first glimpse of Machu Picchu and historic ruins, with a bright blue sky as a backdrop. We were up so high and could see far into the distance and down into the valley we had come from. It was truly spectacular. I couldn't believe I was there up in the clouds. I didn't think I could get any further because of all the steps, but just to get a glimpse was enough for me.

Then the guide said he had employed three men from the village to lift me around the ruins. We set off with the guide calling out 'Make way!' as the men heaved me up and down the narrow steep steps while the guide pointed out places of interest. It was just all so amazing: the scenery, the atmosphere and the culture of a past Inca civilisation.

Over the next few days, we visited temples and ruins and learnt of their culture. The rule of the Incas ended with the invasion of the Spanish Inquisition on their quest to find more gold. I asked if they were angry about this; they said they embraced their mixed culture, as is the case in so many countries now. We tried the local drink made from corn and gave the first drop to the earth to appease the gods.

We drove into the mountains to see the scenery, watch people working their fields, and children coming back from school to their homes in the mountain villages, bringing a herd of cattle with them. We saw women herding sheep along a narrow mountain pass. We watched women weaving the brightly coloured dyed yarns into an assortment of items.

We flew to San Paulo. It was midnight when we arrived. We tried to get a taxi to our hotel in Rio de Janeiro but found a problem. Apparently, the only way to drive to Rio de Janeiro is through a mountain pass, which takes eight hours and cost £200. Also, very few people do this trip as it is too dangerous. The plane had been going on to Rio de Janeiro, which was annoying, but our flight had been booked to San Paulo and return.

We spent ages trying to get a flight, over two hours. No one we approached spoke English, we were met with a lot of shoulder-shrugging when we asked for advice. Eventually, I showed someone at a desk some money; it worked. They came back to me fairly quickly with a couple of tickets for Rio de Janeiro.

At last, we arrived in Rio de Janeiro about 4.00 a.m. and took a taxi to our hotel, only to find it locked and in the dark. We were told to knock loudly as it was not safe to be outside in the dark. The taxi driver left and we felt very vulnerable standing outside in the dark alone.

Suddenly a car screeched to a stop beside us. We pressed ourselves against the glass door, wondering what was going to happen. It was the taxi driver. He decided that it was not safe to leave us alone. Eventually, a light appeared inside and we tumbled into the lobby. The night porter said it was too dangerous to leave the door open, though they were meant to be open day and night. That did it for us. We just didn't feel safe.

We stayed at the hotel for around four days. There were no women working there, everything was done by men, even the cleaning. When walking through the city, we felt as though we were being watched, and later learnt that there was a gang culture going on; no wonder we'd felt so on edge. It explained a lot.

We took a taxi to the base of the Art Deco statue of Christ the Redeemer, towering 98 foot tall at the top of the 2,300 foot Corcovado Mountain. We drove higher and higher through tropical rainforest to the top of the mountain, and then we had to go up three escalators to get to the top. One of the staff just tipped me back and off I went up the escalators. The statue was so huge, with Christ's arms stretching out against the blue sky. We had a clear view of the city below. We also went by cable car to the top of Sugar Loaf Mountain with lovely coastal views.

We walked along the beach, it was winter and fairly deserted. We visited the luxury Copacabana Palace Hotel for a snack. Our sandwiches arrived in silver-topped dishes – very impressive. We sat back and pretended to be rich and famous; then we walked back to the hotel and packed for our return home.

Another memorable, amazing trip.

CHAPTER 56

DANCING WITH MY WHEELCHAIR

I thought that as a disabled person, trussed-up in callipers and a spinal support, I'd never be able to dance.

As I child, I sat on the sidelines watching other people dance. I always felt envious of them while they danced away to the music. They were enjoying themselves, while I was bored. I wore my best smile to please them. I lacked any confidence to try.

At secondary school, our class used a church hall for country dancing lessons. I went with them to sit and watch as they laughed and chatted while trying to learn the dances. I didn't take part in sports or dancing. I either watched them, or read in the library. I knew that many young people went to discos and parties to dance the night away and I couldn't be part of it.

Sometimes our local PHAB club organised a dance. I was with other disabled people and they danced. They wanted me to join in, but I believed I couldn't, and so just watched. After further encouragement, I decided to try. I had to be careful, it was difficult standing and leaning on walking sticks and trying not to lose my balance. I was self-conscious and worried that I might fall over and embarrass myself. When I started to use my wheelchair more, I found it was fun to move to the music and dance.

I joined a wheelchair dance group in Bristol and each week drove the 50 miles to Bristol in the evening to join in. I loved it. We learnt different dances and often took part in dance competitions. After quite a few years, I found the long drive there and back too exhausting, and I had work the next day.

I heard of a line dance group in Yeovil called High Spirits, and contacted them. I started going with another friend, Chrissie, who was also disabled. She'd only recently started using a wheelchair, and I helped her come to terms with her life with a new disability. There were four of us and we met every week to dance the afternoon away. We did displays at the Royal Bath and West Show, danced in the street for Children in Need and proudly wore our line dancing costumes.

In 2007, the group nearly folded. I said that I was willing to take over running the group if we moved the dance group to Taunton, and so High Spirits moved to my hometown. We planned an open day, and on that morning, I heard that my friend Chrissie suffered a stroke and sadly passed away. I'd met her in hospital in the year 2000, and had tried to inspire her to learn to cope with her disability.

Naomi and Tracey came to the open day and wanted to dance, so I set up the group. Geraldine who used to come with Chrissie continued to come as a volunteer. Over 10 years later, we were still dancing. We'd danced at the Sidmouth Folk Festival, busked in the local streets, and visited various places to dance and to try and encourage other disabled people to become involved.

Our dancing evolved. Line dancing involved a lot of quick arm movement which became difficult for some of our dancers. We gradually introduced other dances like the waltz, jive, samba and just dancing to modern music with no arm movements. Some of the dances I acquired from other groups, and other dances I adapted myself.

My friend Izzy loves dancing and when we went on holiday, we danced and twirled around each other, laughing when it didn't go as planned. We often caused a stir on the dance floor. One evening I went with Izzy and some friends to a Medieval Banquet where the wine and cider flowed. This was followed by a disco. I twirled around Izzy and I went to grab Izzy's outstretched arm – and missed, ending up in a heap on the floor. I was soon back in my wheelchair and dancing again.

Until very recently, I held dancing sessions every week, and although our group was small, they were very committed and enjoyed coming. I had never been qualified to teach dancing, I just used my experience and my willingness to adapt. I wanted dancing to be fun. My dancing members could forget any problems they might have for a couple of hours, and spend the afternoon dancing and socialising.

Although I've now given up teaching, I hope to carry on dancing when I can.

CHAPTER 57

REFLECTIONS & GROWING OLDER

Now that I'm older and retired, I still keep busy. I have Post-Polio Syndrome, which means that I'm gradually losing the use of the remaining muscles I have used for so many years in order to cope. I'm finding it harder to transfer, and get tired more easily, so I have to pace myself.

I look back at all the things I have achieved. In some ways, I think I've achieved far more than the average person, through sheer determination to be an equal and live life to the full. I've seen so much of the world, many of the countries I have visited haven't been mentioned in this book.

I have so many friends. We can all record some funny moments together, either on days out or holidays away. Pam and I went to Weston-Super-Mare one day. There's a part of the beach I can stroll on in my wheelchair, when the tide is right. On this occasion, my wheelchair got stuck and I had to be rescued by some willing volunteers. I then accidentally set-off the accessible toilet alarm in a pub, it was really loud, which got everyone running. While walking back to the van, chatting, along the promenade, we didn't realise we were walking towards the land train heading in our direction.

There was a stern look as the train driver rang his bell. Pam said 'It's certainly very different when we go out!'

Full of surprises, always.

I've never really felt angry about becoming disabled and having to use a wheelchair. There was no-one to blame. I only felt angry and frustrated at the way I was sometimes treated, and not being able to participate in many things while growing up.

Sometimes I say to myself: 'What if I hadn't caught polio?' My life might've been very different. I might have got married and had children, but then that can never be taken for granted. I would never had met all my friends, experienced the life I have, and I'm so glad that I met Tim, the love of my life. Life is fine as it is.

In a way, my disability has made me the person I am. I'm a quiet person but my disability has forced me to meet certain challenges. Who would have believed that I could run a Guide Company for nearly twenty years, a PHAB club for ten years, and a wheelchair dance group for over ten years – when I would much rather be in the background.

There have been negative comments made over the years but I would prefer to remember the positive ones. I remember a joke made by a stallholder at the Farmers Market in town while I was strolling by in my wheelchair. He was selling cakes. I told him that I remember my mother buying a lardy cake as a treat when I was a child, and he said: 'Well, you're not that much taller now, are you! Go on, have a treat.' That made me laugh. We could both see the funny side.

I have seen so many improvements for disabled people over the years. I hope that in some small way I have helped toward this, by being very much in the community. I have shown people the need to make alterations. I've often stated what needs to be improved, whether it's an accessible toilet, or handles at the right height, and I'm so happy when people listen to me. The next time I visit, I notice that changes have been made.

Wheelchairs have become so sophisticated now, allowing so many disabled people to become independent. Who would've thought that all new homes these days would have to be built with disabled people in mind! Most of this is all down to changes in attitude, and long may it continue.

When I reached eighteen, my consultant said to me: 'There's nothing more we can do, it's up to you to make the life you want to lead.' I think I have done that. There are still things I want to do and places I'd like to visit.

I recently celebrated my 70th birthday, and I wanted to do something different. Towards the end of November 2019, Helen, Gina, Liz and I flew to Lapland for the week. This holiday couldn't have been more different from my usual travels abroad. We stayed in a lovely self-catering accessible apartment near Övertorneå, in Sweden, near the Arctic Circle. The owner had an accessible minibus and we wrapped-up warm and went out every day, exploring spectacular snow covered scenery with frozen rivers. We strolled through forests, the trees laden with snow. Luckily, my powered wheelchair managed exceedingly well on the compacted snow. The temperature did plummet to -17c on my birthday, the day we saw moose and reindeer. The most exciting day was when we had a husky sleigh ride for an hour through the most wonderful snowy countryside. It made me realise that although I am getting older and slower, I can still enjoy life. I wonder what other adventures might be coming my way in the future?

I often think about why I'd never bonded with my father and stepmother, and had never thought of us as a family. Our life together was a struggle from the time I came out of hospital; there was just nothing there to bring us close together. Was it because I'd spent so long in hospital during my young life, that we never had a chance to get close? Or maybe I found it difficult to relate to a new family. I always felt very much on my own for so much of the time.

It was a great pity that my father and I never managed to have an in-depth conversation about the past, or the way we had coped. He could talk about the weather, recent news and daily tasks, but it was as though he had his own fragile shell around him to hide away from what had happened to our family so that he could handle it.

My parents were there for me, but never expressed any love. I constantly heard what a great effort it was for them, but I never felt special. My friends tell me how my parents expressed to them how proud they were of me; but they'd never told me. I'm glad that I made them proud – that I had succeeded in the life they'd wanted for me.

Parents didn't express love as they do now. They'd been brought up strictly, and so brought up their children through their own experiences; in fact, mine were no different to most other parents of that time. They were not bad people, they both worked hard and did everything they could to make the right decisions. Life was difficult, with constant hospital visits and coping with a society unused to dealing with disabled people. My parents battled endlessly with the local authorities, the hospitals and various establishments to try to give me a better life.

My parents moved from their bungalow to a flat around the year 2000. The flat was near the shops and the doctors, so it was handy for them; and it was accessible to me if I entered through the patio sliding door to the lounge. I was leaving their flat one day and they stood together on the patio waving me goodbye. When a certain distance away, I turned to wave and my mother called out: 'Your father does love you, you know.' I looked at my father – I longed for him to say those words. My heart might've melted a little if he had, but no words came. He just laughed. I heard my mother scold him. I knew he found it hard to express his feelings. Maybe I should've said 'I love you,' but I felt the same. I waved again and went on my way home.

As my parents became older, they learnt to enjoy life more, to be with friends, have holidays and be content with one another. They leaned on each other for support. And I tried to help them, to pay a debt of gratitude for all the years they'd helped me.

My father reached 89 and passed away suddenly. My stepmother attained 90, spending her last few years in a nursing home with ill-health. Towards the end of her life, she said that she was glad she had experienced a purpose in life to bring us together as a family. I nodded in agreement. I felt she had the right to make that claim. We are all who we are, and we can only do our best.

Printed in Great Britain
by Amazon